CURB APPEAL
IDEA BOOK

CURB APPEAL
IDEA BOOK

MARY ELLEN POLSON

The Taunton Press
Inspiration for hands-on living®

The Taunton Press, Inc., 63 South Main Street, PO Box 5506, Newtown, CT 06470-5506
e-mail: tp@taunton.com

EDITOR: Jennifer Matlack
JACKET/COVER DESIGN: Jeannet Leendertse
INTERIOR DESIGN: Lori Wendin
ILLUSTRATOR: Christine Erikson
COVER PHOTOGRAPHERS: Front cover (top row, left to right): © Linda Svendsen,
© Brian Vanden Brink, © 2005 Carolyn L. Bates–carolynbates.com; (middle row, left to right):
© Chipper Hatter, © Brian Vanden Brink, © Lee Anne White, © davidduncanlivingston.com;
(bottom row, left to right): © Erik Kvalsvik, © Lisa Goodman, © Linda Svendsen, © Brian Vanden Brink.
Back cover (top left): © Chipper Hatter; (bottom row, left to right): © Brian Vanden Brink,
© Brian Vanden Brink, © Chipper Hatter.

Taunton Home® is a trademark of The Taunton Press, Inc.,
registered in the U.S. Patent and Trademark Office.

Library of Congress Cataloging-in-Publication Data
Polson, Mary Ellen.
  Curb appeal idea book / Mary Ellen Polson.
     p. cm.
  ISBN-13 978-1-56158-803-9
  ISBN-10 1-56158-803-2
  1. Architecture--Details. 2. Landscape architecture. 3. Outbuildings. 4. Architecture, Domestic--United States. I. Title.
  NA2840.P72 2005
  728'.37--dc22
                     2005015198

Printed in China
10 9 8 7 6 5 4 3 2 1

Acknowledgments

Writing—and reading—about homes and houses can be maddening. You fall in love over and over again and ultimately begin to put bits and pieces of different houses together in your imagination, until everything has evolved into your dream house with enough leftovers to build and furnish a second getaway home.

My editors at The Taunton Press know all about this—they remain calm and reasonable when faced with temptation every day. I'd like to thank all of them for their support and hard work. Special thanks to Carolyn Mandarano, who can cook up an outline for a best-selling book in about 30 seconds, and Jennifer Matlack, who asks such clever questions that she tricks me into rewriting copy without allowing writer's block even to cross my mind. I'd also like to thank others on the editorial team at Taunton, including Julie Hamilton, Jennifer Peters, Maureen Graney, Wendi Mijal, and Sam Peterson.

I'd also like to salute the photographers whose willingness to work with me made this book a thing of beauty: Linda Svendsen, Chipper Hatter, Brian Vanden Brink, Carolyn Bates, David Duncan Livingston, Bob Perron, Bill Wright, Lisa Goodman, and Todd Caverly.

I wouldn't be where I am today without the good folks at *Old House Interiors,* where all of us deal with the stuff of dream houses every day. Special thanks to my friend and editor Patricia Poore and to my much-esteemed colleagues Inga Soderberg, Lori Viator, Sharlene Gomes, Becky Bernie, Joanne Christopher, Julia Hite, and Bill O'Donnell. They have all pulled my fat out of the fire on more than one occasion.

I can't pass up an opportunity to thank the people closest to me, including my husband, Jim; my sister, Anne Johnson, who channeled her love of house hunting into a career as a real-estate broker; and my mother, who is always happy to stay put, no matter where she lives. And I can't resist mentioning my late father, who once picked out a house for our family based on a grainy black-and-white picture in the real-estate section of a newspaper. It had curb appeal, and he bought it.

Contents

Introduction ▪ 2

Chapter 1

Style on the Outside ▪ 4

A Face to the World ▪ 7

Chapter 2

Exterior Appearances ▪ 28

Playing Up Your Best Features ▪ 30

Architectural Elements ▪ 34

Transforming an Exterior ▪ 48

Chapter 3

The Entry ▪ 58

The Front Door ▪ 60

The Right Accents ▪ 72

Landings and Porches ▪ 86

Chapter 4

The Approach ▪ 100

Shaping the Landscape ▪ 102

Walks and Paths ▪ 120

Lighting the Landscape ▪ 130

Chapter 5

Supporting Players ▪ 136

Fences, Walls, and Gates ▪ 138

Driveways ▪ 148

Garages ▪ 156

Resources ▪ 166

Credits ▪ 168

Introduction

When I agreed to write the *Curb Appeal Idea Book* I lived in a house that practically defined curb appeal: It was an adorable brick cottage with a riot of gingerbread trim, a welcoming side porch, and beautiful sidelights around the front door. For personal reasons, I decided to move. And although I've lived in more houses than I can count, my current dwelling is a one-bedroom apartment. It has an incredible view, but the building, a mid-20th-century monolithic slab, definitely comes up short in the curb appeal department.

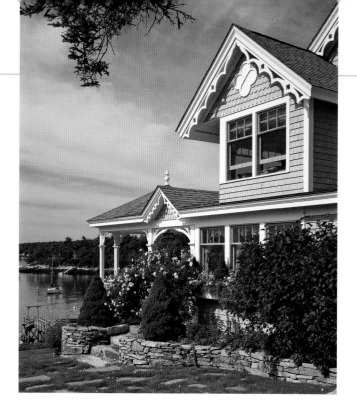

Although I can't change the exterior of my apartment building, you can change the look of your home—whether you own or rent—and the options are all but limitless. Before making plans to change the outside appearance of your home, however, it's a good idea to take some time to decide what you want it to convey. Do you want a new paint scheme that honors its architectural roots? Will updating and enlarging the front stoop provide a more welcoming entry to guests? Are the foundation shrubs planted 40 years ago overgrown and just begging to be replaced?

Even if you are on a tight budget, there are dozens if not hundreds of ways to give the exterior of your home a facelift, whether it's painting just the trim, updating the door hardware, adding container plantings of flowers around the front door, or simply weeding the yard. From curbside to the garage, the front entry, and every place in between, adding curb appeal will create a great first—and lasting—impression of your home. Use the ideas in this book to help you put on the face you want people to see.

Style on the Outside

We all know an appealing house when we see one: Just think of a charming cottage offset by a flourishing garden and bordered by an ancient stone wall. A home that puts on a pleasing "face" appeals to us on many levels, especially psychologically. After all, we have a primal need for shelter and comfort. Some houses are so fetching that they instantly create the desire for possession; it's a well-known real-estate maxim that houses with curb appeal tend to sell more quickly than houses with less-than-stellar looks.

Most of us, however, haven't the time or money to swap houses whenever we spot a home that calls out to us more than our present digs. And with the cost of residential real estate at record highs in many parts of the country, few of us can afford to buy our true dream home: We have to use our ingenuity to transform the space we already have into the home we want. The goal, first and foremost, should be to create a home with a winning appearance for our own enjoyment. Ultimately, if that home appeals to others as well as to ourselves, our efforts may also pay off down the road if we ever decide to sell it.

But suppose you weren't born with the design gene? How do you take a house with "potential" and turn it into a showplace that can turn heads? For starters, acknowledge your house for what it is, whether it's a 1920s Colonial that already has some curb appeal or a 1970s Ranch that needs a complete cosmetic makeover. If it's your home,

◀ NEW TRADITIONAL HOMES please the eye with lots of personalized details. This one incorporates a clipped-gable entry porch and a mix of textures, including staggered shingles on the upper part of the house and clapboard siding below. The deep red window trim complements the primary green ground color.

there must be something about it that won you over. Try to identify the pluses, and be honest with yourself about the minuses.

A good technique to help you spot what's right and wrong with your home's overall appearance is to take pictures. Once you're holding a snapshot of the front of your house (or looking at a digital image on a computer), it's much easier to be objective about its curb appeal—or lack of. Does the front door blend into the walls? Try painting it a color that contrasts with the siding. Do the windows seem to be missing something? Perhaps there should be shutters. Is the yard overgrown with shrubbery? The bottom line: Pictures don't lie.

Look around the neighborhood, too. Since a majority of houses in the United States are at least 30 years old, there may have been some changes made to your home. Your front door may have been altered from the original builder's plans, and perhaps not for the better. Maybe it lost the small covered porch over the entry stoop, for instance. Locating a similar house in your neighborhood that still has its covered entry will help you re-create the original design. In the process of the search, you'll not only meet your neighbors, you might find other design approaches that work equally well toward improving your home.

▲ EVEN SMALL, SIMPLE HOUSES can have plenty of curb appeal. Finished with vertical wood siding, this single-story dwelling gets its sense of playfulness from an unusual circular window and a slightly curving canopy over the front door.

▶ MOST HOUSES have a recognizable architectural style that's made up of elements common to similar houses of the era. The features of this 200-year-old Georgian Colonial include matching, symmetrically spaced windows, a central entry, and an arch and pediment over the door.

▲ THERE ARE MANY WAYS to make a door the focal point of a home. Sometimes all it takes is a bright paint color. This door would have vanished under the shallow front porch if the builder hadn't added a front-facing gable and two columns that frame the entry.

A FACE TO THE WORLD

Every house has a face, or façade. And just as a little lipstick and mascara improve the looks of some people, the right "makeup" can also improve the face of your home. But while cosmetic surgery for a house can be just as expensive and time consuming as, say, a nose job or a brow lift, there's more latitude for trial and error.

Good bones and a unified sense of style are important, too. Most houses—even the plainest or most recently built—have some relationship to a recognizable architectural style such as Cape, Bungalow, Postmodern, or Colonial. All of these styles have identifiable characteristics, from the overall shape of the house to small details like hardware and light fixtures.

▲THE SETTING can be just as important as the house in creating an attractive and cohesive appearance. Here, the pale stucco of the house and walled enclosure create a pleasing backdrop for green louvered shutters and tiered landscaping.

▼ PART OF WHAT MAKES a home appealing is the combination of familiar forms and materials with new ideas, like this vertical window with divided panes of glass. Although the other windows are traditional in appearance, one window offers an innovative twist: It actually pops open from the bottom.

▲ AN UNUSUAL OR RICH primary color can give your home appeal, even when the siding material is mundane or out of date, like these large-scale shingles. Choose a trim color that allows the ground, or main, color to show to best advantage; too much contrast between hues is undesirable.

Before you begin a face-lift, you should know a little about your home's style. Having this information will help you identify the types of elements—windows, doors, roofing materials—that complement the overall architecture of your house. For example, louvered windows that open horizontally by cranking a handle seldom look right on a Cape or Colonial because they were never part of the architectural "package" on these homes, which are based on 200-year-old originals. They may look right at home on your 1960s Ranch, however, because many mid-century houses were designed to include this type of window.

Fitting In with the Neighborhood

I F YOU'RE LIKE MOST AMERICANS, you probably live in a neighborhood where many of the houses were built around the same time and in similar or complementary styles. So if you're planning an exterior makeover, make sure the new look of your home won't jar with the rest of the neighborhood. (Houses that don't fit in can be harder to sell than those that do.)

Start by keeping your house in scale with the homes of your neighbors. If most houses are low story-and-a-half models, for instance, keep your home's new profile low to the ground (you can always add square footage on the back). Another trick is to "borrow" architectural elements from existing houses such as the Victorian gingerbread here and use them in a novel way on your new and improved home.

▲ YOUR HOME SHOULD PRESENT A FACE that's compatible with the surrounding neighborhood. In this enclave, the houses are akin in scale and style, from the triangular gables to small architectural details, like the decorative brackets on the porch posts. A large contemporary, for example, would be an undesirable addition to this quaint neighborhood.

AN APPEALING APPROACH can be as simple as a stone path that meanders from the front door to the side yard. Here, a well-kept exterior, smooth turf, and groupings of well-tended blue hydrangeas complete the picture.

GLOSSY RED PAINT framed by buttery yellow trim draws attention to the vintage details in this Victorian door. Accessories like a period doorknob, gaslight sconces, and plantation shutters in a complementary green reinforce the door as a focal point for the house.

If you're considering adding a second story or converting your home's appearance from one architectural "look" to another (Ranch to Arts and Crafts, for instance), seek help from a building professional or architect. This person will be able to provide valuable information about how to successfully and tastefully accomplish the task. An extreme makeover may increase the square footage of your home, but depending on its execution, you may actually end up with less curb appeal than you had before.

▲ DO YOU VALUE PRIVACY with a personal style that tends toward the clean and contemporary? Clear glass blocks with a rippled finish make a good choice for a sidelight. The glass lets in light but obscures the interior within.

Incorporating Your Personality

Rather than slavishly plan improvements with only the goal of eventual resale in mind, think of your home's exterior as a place to express yourself. Have you always wanted a red house? Perhaps that's the elusive exterior paint color you've been searching for. Did you buy your house because you envisioned window boxes in full bloom under the pic-

ture windows? Then find a carpenter to build them while you select the flowers from a local nursery. Are the posts that support the covered entry kind of boring? Change them to something more substantial, like a three-dimensional column or a whimsical design that reflects your interests. If you're a recreational rower, for example, you might choose posts that suggest the shape of an oar.

▲ IF YOU'RE MAKING OVER
the entry to your home, be
sure to include some personal
touches. Quirky details like the
splayed posts supporting a roof
beam and the curving shape
in the wall give this entry porch
a lot of personality.

▶ IT'S IMPORTANT TO CONSIDER
how your home appears at night.
This entry gains a lot of drama
from the many windows of interesting shapes that allow interior
light to illuminate the exterior
after dark, casting a warm and
welcoming glow.

▲ WITH AN APPROACH framed by a mature oak tree and lush, colorful landscaping, this new Victorian home would be appealing even if the house itself were less than attractive. Luckily, it's beautiful: A broad, welcoming porch and charming architectural details complete the perfect picture.

▲ MUCH OF THE APPEAL of this straightforward frame house lies in its setting—a deep green lawn nestled against a backdrop of dark evergreens. The balanced arrangement of the windows on either side of the front door enhances the overall impression of cozy simplicity.

Another area where you can explore personal tastes is with house accessories such as entry hardware, lighting fixtures, mailboxes, door knockers, even house numbers. Coordinate them to the style of your home or use a single style that you particularly like. Or choose a mix of decorative elements that you think go well together. If your budget is tight, use items that you already have on hand that extend a warm welcome to guests. Are you a whiz with potted plants? Create a display on a porch stoop. Do you collect pottery or straw brooms? Extend your collection out onto the front porch or a covered entry. The idea is to express your own sense of style and personal taste as part of your home's appearance.

▲ SMALL OR UNUSUALLY SHAPED HOUSES can capture positive attention thanks to a bold dose of color. In this case, the bright green shingles
on the façade provide a colorful punch as well as interesting texture to
an otherwise tiny house.

▼ ONE OF THE WAYS architects create appeal
in new structures is by borrowing familiar
architectural elements from older homes and
buildings. The wood siding on this getaway
cabin resembles an old standing-seam "tin" roof.
Painting the siding red—a traditional tin-roof
color—reinforces the effect.

The Impact of Color

Color transforms a house. That's true
whether you change the color of the front
door, repaint the trim, sheath the exterior in
bold new tones, or simply plant vibrant
flowers in your front yard. So it's really up
to you—do you want a subtle change or a
dramatic one?

Before you plunge in, though, there are
a few guidelines to follow when choosing
colors for your exterior. On most homes,
two or three colors look best:

- a ground, or overall, color
- a trim color (for eaves, gables, window
  frames, and the like)
- an accent color (to be applied as a highlight color—for instance, to edge the
  insides of window frames, or on the
  front door)

Since colors always change in relation to
one another, begin by choosing the ground
and trim colors and see how they look
together. The two colors you pick should

▲ THINK OF COLOR as something that happens in your home's landscape, not just on the siding. This Cape-style house with white siding and a gray roof gets all the color it needs from its spectacular front garden.

Variations on a Color Theme

ALTHOUGH THIS SIMPLE WHITE farmhouse has charm, the monochromatic color doesn't do much to enhance details like the porch railing, the porch posts with curving brackets, or the arched window in the attic. Painting the house in a simple two-color combination—red ground with white trim—makes a dramatic difference, accentuating the home's period features. Taking color one step further, however, adds more interest to the home. In this case, creating a three-color scheme is fairly simple: Add dark green on details like the porch railings, brackets, and inside the window frames.

▲ WHITE IS BRIGHT, CHEERFUL, AND TRADITIONAL—but it doesn't do much to show off any period details an older home might have. This century-old farmhouse gets small bursts of color from hanging planters and the Stars and Stripes.

▲ Red with white trim

▲ Red with green and white trim

▲ Details can enhance a color scheme.

▲ A COLOR SCHEME doesn't have to be dramatic to be effective in identifying the key parts of a house. On this attached white farmhouse, red on the front door signals the entry; red also sets the garage apart from the main part of the house.

harmonize and look well together. Since the ground color covers so much of the house, it shouldn't obviously dominate the trim color when you compare the two on paint chips. If possible, use a larger paint chip for the ground color than for the trim color when comparing hues. An even better idea is to test the two colors on a part of the house, exactly as they will appear together. If the trim color is too stark against the ground color (for example, dark purple trim against white), the overall effect may appear harsh and two-dimensional. By selecting ground and trim colors that flatter one another, you can then add a jolt of bold color—deep brick red, rich turquoise, even glossy black—to accent details on the house, like the front door.

Some classic examples of two-color combinations for exteriors include:

- yellow ground color with white trim
- tan ground with white or off-white trim
- white or off-white ground with gray or pale green trim
- medium or sage green ground with gray trim
- warm red or brick red ground with green trim
- navy blue ground with white trim

Some other color ideas include:

- Choose ground and trim colors from the same color family (sage green and forest green, for example). Depending on how pale or saturated the colors are—and whether or not other colors, like black,

▲ MUCH OF THE APPEAL of this welcoming entry comes from the colorful elements that surround it, particularly the window boxes planted with pink and red flowers and a vintage slat chair, now a faded green. There's no missing the door, either—it's bright white.

◄ A BOLD DESIGN often calls for bold color. Although this moss-green ground color is dramatic, it connects the house to the surrounding landscape. The long blue struts supporting the roof are striking, but they also serve a function: They point the way to the entry.

have been added to one or both of them—colors from the same family can appear remarkably different together. You can even add a third variation on green as an accent color, with dramatic results.

- Choose ground and trim colors from opposite sides of the color wheel— yellow and blue, for example, or red and green. The tones don't need to be direct opposites, just a pairing that looks good together. Again, you can play with shades that are lighter or darker than one another. Purer colors, like cherry red, tend to stand out more. On the other hand, a color like pale yellow will appear stronger than a deep shade of tan because it reflects more light.

Color Transforms an Entry

BEFORE BEING TRANSFORMED, this Hacienda Revival-style home in Berkeley, California, had an exterior color scheme that was nothing but bland: The walls, door, and trim were plain white, while the shutters were simply a dark, almost black color. When new owners moved in they decided to punch up the color palette by returning the house to its Spanish roots.

Spanish-style homes in California, Florida, and the Southwest are known for their colorful tiles, which can appear on almost any surface associated with the house—as accents on walls and patios, on the roof, and especially on architectural features like fountains.

The most obvious use of color on the transformed house comes from the tile surrounding the doorway, but other elements—the ceramic planters on either side of the entry, the warm wood tones of the new door, and the wood beams overhead—play a part in enlivening the house as well.

▲ ▶ THIS SPANISH-INFLUENCED HOME had lost much of its original detail and exterior appeal over the years (before photo, left). The new owners revived it with colorful elements—like Moorish-style tiles and wrought-iron hardware—that might once have been on the house.

Adding Color

N O ONE COLOR SCHEME on a home is the "correct" one—all variations will have curb appeal, provided the colors complement one another.

This tropical stucco-sided house is done in variations of light green. The monochromatic color scheme (pale exterior walls with slightly darker trim) would probably work on the house whether the color was pink with rose-colored trim or beige with a pale brown trim, for example.

Another way to vary the color scheme on this house is to keep the trim pale green and match it to a complementary ground color, such as a yellow-tan. For even more drama, a third color can be added; in this case, a dark, almost charcoal black on the shutters and some parts of the window trim.

◀ IT'S HARD TO GO WRONG when you use different shades of the same color to create an exterior color scheme. Stucco houses in warm climates look particularly good in pastels like pale green and pink, or earthy colors such as tan.

▲ Pale orange with green trim

▲ Pale orange with black and green trim

The Entry and Beyond

The approach to a house doesn't begin merely at the front door. It begins when you first see the house from the street. From there, you take in the landscaping, the path to the front door, and the porch or stoop. Any of these elements can be enhanced to increase the curb appeal of your home.

If something on the trajectory to your front door looks out of place, it will affect the overall face of your home. By its nature, curb appeal is hard to define, so it can be helpful to break down the various aspects into recognizable components. They include exterior elements, the entry, the approach, and supporting players.

▼ IN SOME HOMES, curb appeal is apparent whether you're outside or just inside the front door. As you look out through an entry framed by leaded-glass sidelights, this home presents a pleasant vista across a well-groomed lawn to a boat-filled harbor.

▲ AS WE APPROACH A HOUSE, we pass through a series of different elements, which can make or break the appeal of a home. Here, a walkway through the front lawn, the steps up to the fenced enclosure, the stoop, and the brightly colored front door are all handsome parts of a larger, attractive whole.

▲ DON'T OVERLOOK the impact that plants and trees can play in increasing your home's curb appeal. A large part of the beauty of this setting comes from a mature tree: Its spreading branches softly frame the house and the entire front yard.

▶ NOT EVERY attractive home begins with a door front and center. This Asian-influenced home gets a lot of its appeal from subtle landscaping and a waterfall pouring over a wall. In addition to being a pleasing focal point, the wall also provides privacy for the front of the house.

Exterior elements are all of the architectural features on the front of the house that affect its appearance, from the bricks or siding to the roof and the windows. Changing different aspects of the façade can greatly enhance your home's curb appeal, as the makeovers in chapter 2 should demonstrate. Chapter 3 hones in on the entry itself—an area that includes not only the front door and important accessories like entry hardware and lighting but also the steps, stoops, and porches that lead to it. The fourth chapter expands the idea of curb appeal to the front yard, including the landscaping, paths, and walkways that lead to the house. Finally, we'll consider garages, driveways, fences, walks, and gates. Often overlooked but very important because of their size, these supporting players can often make or break a home's curb appeal.

▲ AN ENTRY UNDER a shallow porch roof offers plenty of opportunity for enhancement. Columns or posts used as supports can be placed so that they frame the entrance. Here, a light blue ceiling, which suggests the sky, makes the porch seem more expansive.

▲ PART OF WHAT MAKES an entry beautiful is how it fits in with the rest of the façade, or front of the house. Here, the windows repeat the lovely arch over the front door, which creates a sense of harmony on the exterior of the home.

◄ REPEATING ARCHITECTURAL ELEMENTS— like arches within arches, or a gable recessed into a larger gable on the front of the house—makes the approach to a house interesting as well as attractive. Elements such as these also add a sense of proportion to the dwelling.

Defining Lines

HOME IS A PRIVATE refuge, but its exterior is open to the world. Elements like fences, front porches, and even simple entry stoops help define the separation between what's private and what's on view to the neighbors. Fences, especially, make the demarcation between public and private property clear—although it's customary that front-yard fences are easy to see through or low enough to see over. That's because the front yard is part of the streetscape and neighborhood, at least visually. It serves as a friendly buffer between the public way and the private interior of the house. In other words, you can feel right at home greeting a neighbor over the fence from your yard, but you don't necessarily have to invite anyone in.

▶ PROTECTED BY A spindled iron fence and a broad front porch, this gingerbread Victorian presents an attractive face to the world. At the same time, the fence, flight of steps, and imposing porch railing afford plenty of privacy.

◀ SOME HOUSES have more than their share of charming features. This one boasts a pretty bay-front window, a vine-covered entry porch, a pleasing color scheme, and a more subtle architectural element—a gable within a gable.

Exterior Appearances

A house is a complicated piece of architecture. Not only is it three-dimensional, but it's also made up of a host of major components, from the foundation to the roof. The front of a house is called the façade, and anything and everything that can be seen from the street—the siding, roof, windows, front door, and supporting features like shutters—plays a role in how your home is perceived by others. Understanding how these components work together is the key to creating a home with true curb appeal.

Making the most of your home's exterior appearance can be a simple matter of changing the paint color, altering the siding, or adding a new window or front door. On the other hand, the front of your house may be a candidate for serious rethinking: It may require a comprehensive makeover, such as expanding the front porch to create an outdoor room, and change the entire look of the façade.

No matter how you improve your home, however, it's important to create a unified, overall appearance for your home's "face" so it looks its very best.

◄ STUCCO DOESN'T have to be white or pastel in color. On this sage-green stucco house, trim possibilities range from dark forest greens to rich brick red. The owners chose a soft brown that is only slightly darker than the ground color.

Playing Up Your Best Features

ALL HOUSES HAVE A SENSE of style. These days, however, architectural elements are combined with so much abandon that it can be hard to pin down exactly what style your home is. For example, a Ranch house could easily have Colonial features like a fanlight and window shutters while a Cape might have a front porch trimmed with Victorian millwork.

No matter. Whether you consider your home traditional or contemporary, it's more important that the house project a sense of flair that's pleasing to you. While it can be helpful to add details or paint colors that are characteristic of an identifiable style (such as white with black shutters on a 1920s Colonial), allow yourself the freedom to be creative. That means choosing materials, colors, and textures that both complement the look of your house and express your personal style. Maybe that white Colonial would look even better with a lavender front door. It's all a matter of working with what you've got—and doing what you like.

MORE TRADITIONAL than contemporary, this impressive home mixes a variety of bold textures and fanciful architectural features, like a three-sided tower and an eyebrow window in the slate roof. Windows grouped in threes help unify the exuberant façade.

THIS HOUSE PROJECTS a sense of style that's neither old nor new but a little bit of both. While the lines are crisp and contemporary, the house is finished with shingles used three different ways— a technique borrowed from late 19th-century homes.

THE EXTERIOR OF A HOUSE doesn't have to be fancy to have curb appeal. The charm of this simple home lies in a single unifying color. The steps are clean and uncluttered, and vertical battens on the siding provide some relief.

MAKING A STATEMENT

▲ SMALL TOUCHES TO A HOUSE can add a lot of charm. These wishbone-shaped brackets underneath a deep eave demonstrate just that. The brackets not only frame the corner window, but also subtly point to the flower box just underneath it.

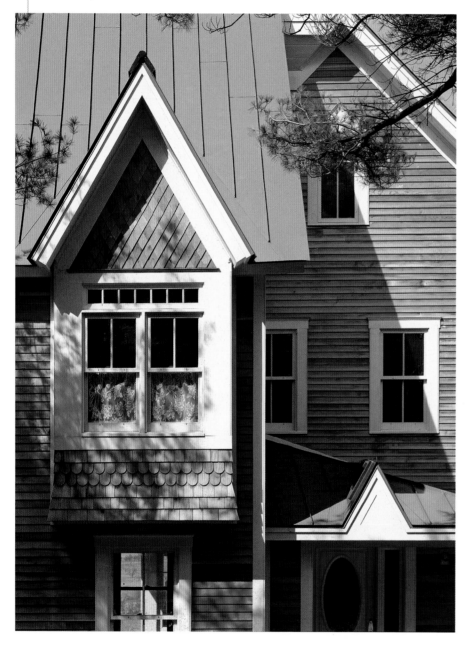

▲ STRONG ARCHITECTURAL FEATURES like a tin roof and natural-finish shingles and siding make this home a standout. A large part of its appeal comes from the careful positioning of the windows—two underneath the peaked gable in the bump-out and two framing the peak in the porch roof.

▲ THIS STUCCO HOUSE gains tremendous visual impact from bold, propped-out Bermuda shutters that double as sun guards. While traditional shutters emphasize the shape and positioning of windows, these emphasize the flowing lines of the roof, making the house seem larger.

▲ A BROAD VERANDA with a low-pitched roof makes a bold statement and makes this one-story house seem much larger. Deep porches are an excellent way to increase your home's curb appeal. In effect, they add an extra room to the house, which is especially ideal in warm locales.

◄ HOMES RIGHT ON A ROAD often turn a blind face outward. But that doesn't mean your home can't be attractive. This homeowner finished the front with narrow battens and repeated them overhead in exposed rafter tails. Latticework with lush greenery adds a cool color and softens the exterior.

Architectural Elements

WHEN YOU LOOK AT THE exterior of your home, what do you see? The largest, most obvious elements are the siding or cladding, the roof, and the windows. If you focus your energies on making sure these components look good both individually and together, you will greatly enhance your home's appearance.

It's easy to take the siding for granted, whether it's brick, wood, stone, metal, or stucco. But don't make that mistake! You can always change the color of the cladding and the trim around windows and doors or choose different textures (for example, rough stucco versus smooth). The roof is equally important: It can easily make up half of what the eye sees on a home's exterior. As for windows, it's important that they are well sized and positioned; a poorly placed or ill-sized window can make the entire face of a house look off-kilter.

◀ THE MAJOR ELEMENTS— roofing, siding, and windows —all work together to give this cottage an inviting, unified appearance. The roof, windows, and covered entry porch are all outlined with painted green trim—a trick that helps to pull the façade of a house together.

◀ TUCKED AWAY UNDER AN EAVE, a window with shutters gets a lift from a bracketed window box filled with flowers. The lavender supports do their part to create unity on the home's façade: They match the decorative brackets on a slight recess at the second-story level.

▲ THE STEEPLY PITCHED ROOF on this house dominates it in terms of style. Adding some charm and relief, however, are the diamond-paned windows and the peaked entry porch. Without these two important features, the roof would have been too much of an overpowering presence.

◀ A CONTEMPORARY DESIGN can look as though it has always been part of the landscape. Traditional building shapes like a sloping gabled roof and a shed porch reinforce the sense of past times, as do the unfinished shingles, a staple of early American homes.

SIDING AND CLADDING MATERIALS

▲ NOT ALL BRICK IS FLAT RED, as this home with its pinkish hues demonstrates. Manufacturers today offer brick in a wide range of colors and textures, with different blends available to suit any style of home, from traditional to the boldest contemporaries.

► A CLASSIC SIDING TREATMENT for early American homes is wood siding. Called clapboards, these are long, narrow boards installed horizontally across the face of the house. The boards are painted and overlap so that water will run off of them.

▲ TRADITIONAL IN HOT-WEATHER CLIMATES
like the Southwest, stucco is an increasingly
popular finish material for new homes today.
Its smooth, subtle texture can suit a minimalist
contemporary or serve as a backdrop for styles
with a lot of decorative detail, like Neo-Spanish
Colonial. Like wood, it can be painted any color.

▲ NATURALLY FINISHED WOOD is an attractive siding material for a contemporary home.
The earthy color of the wood marries well with other natural materials, like stone, and helps
tie the entire house to the surrounding landscape.

Choosing Cladding

UPGRADING THE SIDING ON your home is one
way to improve its appearance. The most
traditional choice is horizontal lap wood
siding in cedar, redwood, or white pine. (Occasionally, wood siding is installed vertically and finished
with battens, narrow strips that conceal the
seams.) Alternatives include wood composites;
these man-made boards are less expensive than
real wood siding.

Other traditional cladding materials include
shingles, which can be painted, stained, or left natural, and brick. Brick is more expensive than wood,
but it never rots or needs painting.

Vinyl and aluminum, the least-expensive siding
choices, are frequently installed as original siding
on new houses today, often in a durable factory
finish in the color of your choice. Although either
material will last practically forever, the color fades
and needs to be repainted after about 10 years.
Both materials tend to show dirt more easily than
wood, too.

If you prefer a romantic, Old World appearance,
stucco and natural or synthetic stone are good
choices but tend to be more expensive than other
siding options.

▲ RICHLY TEXTURED BRICK STEPS
create a pleasing contrast for a
stucco house tinted a rosy pink.
Two bump-outs on either side
of the front door help to frame
the entry; the walkway centered
on the door reinforces the sense
of balance.

◄ SMALL DETAILS, like a lattice
that conceals the exterior crawl
space on this shingled house,
are important finishing touches
that keep the overall appearance
of a house neat and clean. Paint
a finishing piece like this in a
related or contrasting color.

RED IS A GREAT COLOR for siding. It looks good (and very different) whether it's paired with light or dark trim. It's also easy to match to a broad range of colors, especially those in the green family.

▲ A LOG HOME in a natural finish offers plenty of rough-hewn charm. Infill panels made of sapling-sized sticks add extra texture under a bay window, while crisp green paint on the trim gives the façade a little polish.

Siding Colors

JUST ABOUT ANY COLOR under the sun can work as a primary ground color on the exterior of a home. That said, some materials lend themselves to certain color palettes. Stucco, for example, looks best in a range of earth colors, from whites and pastels to greens and browns. Brick varies naturally depending on the type of clay in the mix, from light pinks and tans to deep reds and browns. While wood siding can be painted, it can also be stained or left natural, as can shingles, which weather to an attractive silver-gray if left untreated.

In addition to white, red and green are the ground colors that give the most latitude in picking a complementary trim color. Blues, on the other hand, are notoriously difficult to match.

THE ROOF

▲ THE SUPPORTS that hold up a roof are called rafters. Exposing the ends of the rafters is a wonderful way to add interest to the area under the roof. These rafter tails have been shaped with a saw to resemble the heads of horses.

▲ IT'S POSSIBLE TO ENLIVEN A ROOF without replacing the shingles or painting the eaves. This shingled cottage gets a burst of color from a climbing wisteria, which cascades over the edge of the roof from crest to gutter.

◄ PROVIDED IT'S KEPT PAINTED to avoid rusting, a standing seam metal roof can be an attractive and exceptionally long-lived roof. Versatile enough for most styles of homes, the base material is steel, copper, or aluminum. The standing seams are created with a crimping machine.

Roofing Materials

Y EARS AGO, ASPHALT SHINGLES were a foregone conclusion as the roofing material of choice on American homes. Although they're still popular, today's asphalt shingles come in a host of variations. Some have slightly varied overlap patterns to make them look more "architectural" and others have shadow lines to make them look like clay tiles. Still others are textured to resemble hand-split cedar shakes.

Other traditional roofing options include barrel-vaulted clay tiles and thick, substantial slate tiles. You can find good value in look-alikes made of concrete or metal, though, which resemble the higher-priced traditional choices.

While most roofing materials are available in earth tones, the color possibilities may surprise you, ranging from almost black to red and orange, plus green and yellow.

Concrete

Clay

Metal

Slate

▲ ROOFING MATERIALS are surprisingly diverse these days. In addition to the ubiquitous asphalt shingle, there are concrete shingles that resemble asphalt and metal tiles that look like clay, as well as traditional materials like barrel-vaulted clay tiles and slate shingles.

WINDOWS

▲ WINDOWS THAT CRANK OPEN from the bottom are called jalousy windows. Arranged in a vertical bank of six on a contemporary house, these windows let in plenty of air but not rain. The angle also repeats the slant of the metal roof.

▲ A TRIPLE WINDOW IS A VERY OLD, very stylish combination. This triple window over an entry not only adds interest to the house, but also echoes the arrangement of sidelights around the front door. The lack of grillwork (or muntins) on the lower panes reinforces the home's Arts and Crafts style.

◄ RATHER THAN THINK of windows as single units, imagine the possibilities when they're paired up in twos, threes, or fours. Although these windows are small and narrow, together they create a large, picturesque span that lets in a lot of bright light.

Window Types

THERE ARE SEVERAL BASIC WINDOW TYPES that make good style choices for a majority of homes. The first is the colonial-style window. These tall, well-proportioned windows line up in rows horizontally and vertically, and are evenly spaced around the front door. Each window is double hung, meaning there are two individual sashes. Each sash is divided into individual panes by a grid. Colonial windows usually have at least six panes per sash, top and bottom.

A second window type is the Arts and Crafts window. These windows can also be double hung, but only the top sash is divided into individual panes (usually with four or six panes of glass). Arts and Crafts windows are often grouped in rows of three or more.

Contemporary windows tend to be large pieces of plate glass. While they can be any size, it's still important to align them in rows.

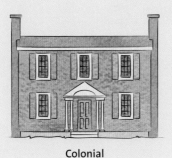

Colonial

Arts and Crafts

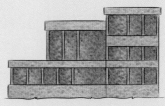

Contemporary

Shutter Styles

SHUTTERS DRESS UP A **window.** The traditional shutter comes in pairs, with one shutter placed on either side of a window. Shutters can be louvered (vented slats), paneled (solid with some relief), or board and batten (a rustic style). It's also possible to personalize shutters by cutting whimsical shapes—diamonds, acorns, or quarter moons, for example—into the bottom panel.

Whereas louvered or paneled shutters are usually fixed in place, Bermuda shutters pop open like an awning over a window. Bermuda shutters can be louvered or constructed of vertical boards. In addition to supplying protection from hot sun in warm climates, they also protect windows during storms when closed.

▲ NOT ALL SHUTTERS swing open at the side. In warm climates or seaside locations, Bermuda shutters traditionally open from bottom to top to create shade and let in breezes. They lock down to protect the house during bad weather or for winterization.

◄ A PLAIN WINDOW on a simple house can take on charm with the addition of shutters and a well-filled flower box. Choosing flower colors that complement or match the color of the house will intensify the impact of the display.

▼ SIDE SHUTTERS are a throwback to Colonial times, when many windows didn't have glass in them. Today's shutters, however, are mostly decorative and are fixed in place. Even so, they can create a lot of impact on traditional homes, which can look bare and naked without them.

▶ VICTORIAN HOUSES **offer** both the charm of gingerbread millwork and large, sunny windows—traits that make the style a popular one to copy today. Pairing up windows in twos and threes goes a long way in opening and flooding the interior of a home with warm, natural light.

◀ WINDOWS ARE USED lavishly on this English country-inspired home to bring in light and add charm. The tall vertical windows fit nicely into the scheme that uses half-timbering on the top story, while the attractive details called quoins accent the smaller windows.

DETAILS

▲ PLAY UP THE ROMANTIC possibilities of your house with details. Here, projecting rafters exaggerate the line of the roof. This technique—a favorite used on Arts and Crafts houses— also creates a good spot for a hanging light fixture.

▲ DON'T OVERLOOK the possibilities for decoration on large pieces of house trim like gutters and downspouts. Here, a decorative plate with a floral pattern adds a bit of flair without adding substantial cost.

▲ THE EXPOSED RIVER ROCK on the chimney of this cottage is a romantic, whimsical detail typical of Arts and Crafts homes that would be easy to incorporate into the design for a chimney on a newer house.

▲ DECKS, PORCHES, and even latticework covering a raised basement can benefit from a unified approach to design. The top section of the porch railings repeats the square grid of the latticework, while arched trusses soften the impact of all the straight lines.

◄ STONE IS A traditional foundation material, but these rounded boulders are just for show—an inventive way to cover a crawl space. Lattice, low-growing shrubs, and tinted concrete are a few other ways to conceal or even beautify an unsightly, exposed foundation.

Transforming an Exterior

AN EXTERIOR MAKEOVER CAN BE a challenging process. But if you really believe the front of your house needs more than just a new coat of paint, a comprehensive transformation is well worth tackling. Before you begin, though, be sure to identify what the problem areas are and the steps (and cost) required to fix them.

Do you want to expand space on the second floor? You'll need to consider the impact of raising the roof by a half or full story. Are the windows in poor condition or ill-suited to the house? Now may be the time to rethink their size and placement. Or perhaps you simply want to add a front porch. If so, you'll probably need to rethink the roofline as well.

Exterior makeover projects are not for the fainthearted. To make the process easier, arm yourself with a good plan, a good designer or architect, and a builder who comes with sterling recommendations from friends or neighbors.

▲ PLACED IN THE CENTER OF THE HOUSE, the new entry is protected by a broad, welcoming porch. The owners also kept and refreshed ideas from the original house, like the door sidelights and curving entry steps.

◄ ALTHOUGH THE APPROACH to this house is attractively trimmed with a brick walk and shrubbery, the house has a dated appearance, thanks to its 1950s-style wide-board siding.

▼ SOME MAKEOVERS are subtle. The exterior colors haven't changed much, and the roof pitch is still low. But the eaves are deeper and the roofline more varied, with overhangs where they're needed most. New window arrangements also let far more light into the house.

▶ **THE MOST CHARMING ASPECT** of this Bungalow before it was remodeled was its attractive roofline, which featured decorative brackets. The architect–owner opted not to alter the existing roofline, which would have destroyed much of the home's appeal.

Rethinking the Roof

R AISING THE ROOF CAN BE A GOOD WAY to increase the size of your home. While adding a full second story can effectively double the square footage in your house, you may find the price tag prohibitive. A second option is to raise the roof by a half story. Since many homes already have the equivalent of half a story on hand in the form of an unfinished attic, this option can be quite attractive from a cost standpoint. The trade-off is usually in lost interior headroom where the roofline slopes downward. To bring in light, you'll need to bump out the roof in certain places, either with windows or a secondary gable.

One-and-a-half story with dormers

Single story

One-and-a-half story with cross gable

▲ WHEN THE OWNER ADDED ON from the bottom up, he not only increased the square footage by a third but also enhanced his home's curb appeal. Attractive new elements include the two-sided entry stair and shingled siding on the ground floor.

RAISING THE ROOF

◀ THE OWNERS of this plain 1940s Ranch house were looking for a complete style makeover as much as extra space. The low roofline didn't allow much room for an attic expansion, and the house lacked a real front porch.

▼ CHANGING THE PROFILE of the roof to a higher, end-gable style created enough room for a new second story. The new design transformed the house from a Ranch into a cottage, complete with a romantic sitting porch under the new, sloping roof.

Roof Dormers

A DORMER—A BUMP-OUT IN the roof that includes a window—can add a lot of charm to the face of your home. If you're expanding into an attic or second story, you can maximize the impact of these handy bump-outs in one of two ways. The first is simply to double or even triple the size of the dormer (from one window to three, for example). The second is to add a dormer in the form of a cross gable, a secondary roof that's installed perpendicular to the main roof. Both methods have the effect of making the exterior of the house appear more substantial. The interior space will be brighter and feel roomier, too.

▲ THIS DORMER IS TUCKED into a cross gable, a secondary roof that's turned perpendicular to the main roof profile. This one is centered right over the front door, creating a focal point for the house.

▶ WHILE THIS CAPE certainly has plenty of curb appeal, it's easy to understand why the owners wanted to expand it. Despite a side room with a bay-front window, the house looks like it's small and dark on the interior.

Figuring Proportions

HERE'S A GOOD REASON why you should consider hiring an architect if you're going to add on to your home: He or she is trained to work with building shapes and proportion.

As you think about the size and scale of your project, however, it may help to know about the Golden Section, a simple mathematical calculation for figuring out the proportions of an addition. For example, say the front of your house is 48 ft. wide (a). Divide 48 by the magic number (known as *phi* to architects): 1.618. A house width of 48 ft. divided by 1.618 results in a segment 29.66 ft. long (b). That's not quite two-thirds of the existing width of your house. If your new addition is about 29.66 ft. long, its proportions will look in scale with the existing house.

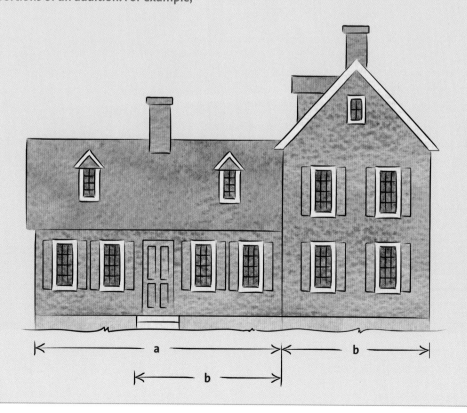

▲ THE OWNERS ADDED A SIDE ADDITION to the house, extending the roofline and raising it slightly. This allowed for a covered porch and a string of attractive dormers on the second floor, each with its own miniature roof.

RETHINKING THE PORCH

◀ THIS SINGLE-STORY HOME doesn't project much of a personality. It's hard to tell where the entry is, and the windows don't line up, making the house look clumsy and out of balance. The owners decided to address several issues with a porch addition.

▼ ALTHOUGH THE PROFILE and roofline of the house haven't changed much, the overall look of the house has improved dramatically. The new porch has become a focal point, and the windows not only line up, but also add character to different parts of the house.

▶ ADDING ON TO YOUR HOUSE doesn't necessarily mean building a lot of enclosed square footage. Although this Cape-style cottage is charming, the front deck looks out of place, and the entry has no protection from the weather.

▼ WRAPPING THE SMALL HOUSE at right in a big front porch is a cost-effective way to increase living space. The new porch protects the entry from inclement weather and is a delightful place to relax in the shade during balmy weather.

The Entry

Nothing goes further toward creating good feelings for a home than an attractive front door. But there's much more to an inviting entry passage than a mere portal. For one thing, the entry must be a strong focal point, so visitors know where to enter. That's the reason so many doors are placed front and center on a house.

At the same time, the entry marks a division between public and private space. A successful entry offers a pleasing face to passersby yet maintains interior privacy for you and your family. For that reason, it's important to consider other elements beyond the door— the door frame, sidelights, stoops and steps, covered entries, and larger porches—when evaluating your entry. Large or deep entry porches, for example, not only protect the front door from inclement weather, but they can darken interior spaces. If your home has one of these, you may want to add glass in or around your door to brighten things up.

Details are especially important around the entry, too. Hardware, lighting, plants, and additional items like screen doors can all have a tremendous impact on an entry's overall appearance.

◄ PAINT THE CEILING on a deep porch a light color to help reflect more light into the house. Light blue is traditionally found on porch ceilings, in part because it mimics the sky but also because the shade helps to reduce glare.

The Front Door

THE DOOR TO YOUR HOME is probably the first thing any guest or visitor sees. Even if the door isn't attractive on its own merits, there are many ways to enhance that important first impression. Positioning is key: Most doors should be centered between other large architectural elements, like windows, columns, or a covered entry porch, to create a sense of importance. If the door is on the side of the house, it helps to have strong elements that point to it—side panels or an entry porch, for instance.

The door itself should be distinctive. If the style isn't particularly impressive, paint the door an attractive color. It's perfectly fine to use bold hues like red, black, or even lavender on the front door, provided you don't go overboard with color elsewhere on the front of the house. Key the style of the door to the overall style of your home (traditional, contemporary, or rustic). If need be, you can also simply replace the door!

▲ SOME DOOR DESIGNS are especially friendly and welcoming. This paneled wood door features a bank of window panes at the top that resembles a traditional sash window. Supporting details include a horizontal "sill" underneath the panes, plus block details.

◀ A FRONT DOOR recessed into the side of an arched opening might be hard to spot. For that reason, the owner has added a pretty, arched-shaped trellis covered with vines to alert visitors to its presence.

▲ THIS ENTRY DOOR in warm wood is highly successful because so much of what leads to it is attractive. A covered entry and a set of railings are both painted a clean, crisp white. Landscaping touches, including a climbing vine over the porch lantern and potted plants in full bloom soften the architecture and add color and texture.

◄ ALTHOUGH THE DOOR is rather plain, other features on this house make it a desirable focal point. The entry is flanked on either side by matching windows with shutters and window boxes, and the door is centered under a peaked gable, painted a soft green.

TRADITIONAL ENTRY DOORS

▲ FORMAL DOORS are often symmetrically balanced. To achieve this kind of look, use elements in threes and fives. This Arts and Crafts–style entry has five panels and three leaded-glass windows. Another way to create symmetry is to place light fixtures or potted plants on either side of the door.

◄ A PANELED DOOR in a beautiful and long-lived wood like mahogany gives a house a sense of solidity and formality. To increase the door's presence, this one is trimmed with an arched surround that includes sidelights and a spiderweb-patterned fanlight over the entire entry.

◄ THIS COLONIAL HOME has two entries: the formal one in the center, and a side entrance facing the driveway that is probably used more often. Both entries share similar traditional characteristics, like formal trim work and side lights.

Sidelights

ONE WAY TO BRIGHTEN a doorway and give it more importance is to add sidelights, vertical panels of glass that run on each side of a door frame. Sidelights (a light is the architectural term for a pane of glass) help to illuminate a front room or entry hall without sacrificing privacy, especially if the glass is patterned or colored, as with leaded glass. They also tend to add balance and proportion to an entry, so they're often used when the front door is a side entry rather than a center one.

Sidelights can be paired with an arched fanlight or a horizontal glass panel over the door, called a transom. The width of the transom can match the width of the sidelights, or it can be narrower or wider—whatever makes the entry look most balanced.

ART GLASS LETS IN LIGHT but maintains privacy by keeping out prying eyes. Here, leaded-glass sidelights in a flowering-tree pattern enliven an Arts and Crafts entry door. The transom is about half the width of the sidelights, which creates a sense of harmony and balance.

Door Types

RAISED PANEL DOORS ARE PROBABLY the most familiar door style. The door gets its name from the pairs of vertical panels that seem to "float" between the flat cross and side pieces that hold them in place. There are usually four or six panels to a door.

Arched doors are often composed of a rounded raised panel at the top and a rectangular panel at the bottom. The arched shape lends itself well to paired doors.

A cottage-style door has two or three narrow vertical panels at the bottom and one or more panes of glass at the top. Suitable for many types of houses, cottage doors lend themselves to inserts of leaded glass and additions like transoms and sidelights.

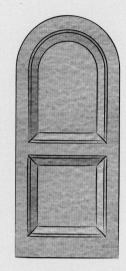

Raised panel   Arched   Cottage style

▶ IF YOUR FRONT door is strongly one style, embellish it with other characteristics of that style. This Victorian entry is enriched by an abundance of Victorian features, including a leaded glass front door, an elaborate, horseshoe-arched screen, and a cascade of flowering plants. Amidst purple hues, the light brown door is an unmistakable standout.

▼ THIS TRADITIONALLY STYLED entry door is not only attractive but wheelchair accessible, too. The key to accessibility is to eliminate any steps on the approach and to minimize any height variations between the exterior decking, the interior floor, and the threshold. The door opening should also be at least 36 in. wide.

▲ THE IDEA OF a broad horizontal beam framing an entryway comes from classical Greek architecture. Although this side entry door is already well-proportioned and balanced by sidelights, the temple-like shape adds an extra measure of formality.

▶ CLASSICAL FORMS LIKE ARCHES are also traditional for front doors. The arch over this entry is repeated in the Spanish-style arch in the roofline. A lantern hung high over the door reinforces the sense of balance.

▲ TRADITIONAL DOESN'T ALWAYS mean formal. This door, recessed under a porch, is especially welcoming because the glass panes repeat the two-over-two pattern of the sash windows. A hand-chiseled granite column adds an element of surprise.

▶ WHEN THE DOOR and siding material are similar in tone or color, use bold or bright trim to increase the visibility of the entry. The blue-gray trim surrounding the doorway makes this traditional Arts and Crafts door stand out.

◄ A FANLIGHT is a glass panel over the door in the form of a shallow arch. Fanlights, like columns, are another way of adding formality to an entry. This one has the extra twist of appearing under the covered entry porch rather than directly over the door.

Door Color

DOORS CAN BE PAINTED, stained, or sealed to let the natural beauty of the wood shine through. Almost any color can be used, since you want the door to call attention to itself.

White, black, and red have always been popular choices, but for the venturesome, choose a bold color that complements your cladding or siding, including greens, yellows, blues, or even startling colors like purple or lavender.

If you'd rather have a rich or bold color on your siding instead of the door, paint the door the same color as the trim. Use a glossy paint, preferably enamel. Early American doors are often treated to multiple coats of high-gloss enamel paint, with a sanding in between each layer, until the finish is so smooth and shiny that you can almost see your reflection in it.

▲ BECAUSE RED ADDS WARMTH to the façade of a home and goes so well with many colors, it is an excellent choice for a front door. This example stands out clearly against the white siding and is a natural complement for the blue shutters.

CONTEMPORARY AND RUSTIC ENTRY DOORS

▲ ALTHOUGH THE STYLE of this door is contemporary, it does many of the traditional things we expect a door to do: It lets light in through its grid of rectangular glass panes, yet is difficult to see through. To ensure total privacy within the foyer of your home, use colored, leaded, or frosted glass.

▲ WOOD ADDS WARMTH to any house, especially when the door is in the form of naturally finished vertical planks with exposed knots. A rectangular panel of glass adds a touch of delicacy to the rough lines of the door and lets in some light.

▲ THE ENTRY ON THIS LOG HOME uses the traditional form of a raised-panel door but with playful materials—tree bark on the panels, stick dividers in the arched fanlight, and a bone door handle. The mix of natural textures adds interest to what could have been an otherwise simple wood door.

◄ OVERSIZED AND completely flat, this entry door echoes the use of rectangular panels of glass elsewhere in this mid-century Modern house. The door is not completely plain, however. The entry hardware is substantial and a shiny metal kick panel, which protects the bottom of the door, adds a bit of flash.

▼ THE EARLIEST AMERICAN
doors were crude affairs, made
of rough-hewn boards held
together by cross pieces, often
without nails. A vertical glass
panel slightly off-center in this
plank door gives it a more contemporary appearance.

▲ COMBINING DIFFERENT TEXTURES can be a good way to make an entry eye-catching. A door
framed by peeled logs seems perfectly in keeping with a house trimmed with rough-cut siding,
columns made of stone, and a pebbled entry porch. Interesting details include a grate over a
square peep-hole.

▲ EVEN AN ENTRYWAY with plenty of concrete can incorporate the formal ideas of balance and symmetry. Here, concrete walls enfold the courtyard, and concrete pillars and glass sidelights frame the entry door. A jazzy metal pergola arched at an angle overhead puts a contemporary spin on things.

◄ A FORMAL DOOR can seem rustic with the right finish treatment. Although this entry is composed of a pair of arched paneled doors, the streaky green paint color (created by layering different shades of paint for effect) gives it an aged, well-worn appearance.

The Right Accents

SMALL DETAILS can make the difference between a doorway that shines and one that simply falls flat. Once you've carefully chosen a new front door or livened up your old door with a fresh coat of paint, give just as much consideration to essentials like entry hardware, the lighting over or beside the door, and any other accents that fall within the immediate vicinity, from porch furniture and flower pots to door numbers and the mailbox.

The one door accessory that's most often overlooked is the storm/screen door (a door frame with interchangeable screen and glass panels). If you have a metal storm door with an initial on it from the family who lived in your home 40 years ago, it's probably time to replace it with a new one more in keeping with the style of the house. Screen doors can either be metal or wood, and they lend themselves to a variety of styles.

▲ ENRICHMENTS CAN BE ADDED to doors where you least expect them. This paneled mahogany door in a warm, natural finish becomes something out of the ordinary with the addition of carvings of local ground covers and wildflowers. Although this door is custom made, you may be able to get something similar from a high-end door maker.

◄ FOR THE SAKE of delivery people and new visitors, most house numbers should be at least 4 in. high so that they are easy to read from the street. Many stylish options abound, from traditional numbers like these to ceramic and metal versions in a variety of styles, from Art Deco to Arts and Crafts.

◄ THE RIGHT LIGHT FIXTURE creates a safe and inviting approach to any home. Choose outdoor fixtures that complement the particular style of your home—black iron lantern styles for Early American homes, hammered metal and art glass for Arts and Crafts homes, and sleek metal for modern houses, for example.

▲ SELECTIVELY PLACED VINES or shrubs like this climbing rose can reward you with an entry that is particularly inviting. A vine-shaded arbor is an attractive solution for entries that get full sun but lack a porch. Here, a cozy seat, an almost transparent screen door, and a lantern sconce enhance the sense of welcome.

SCREEN DOORS

▶ A SCREEN DOOR can be painted to match the trim on the main door or, if it will be taken down in the winter, painted in an alternate color. A striking color, like the dark green used here, makes the door stand out.

▶ COUNTRY HOUSES and farmhouses practically beg for a screen door. This example with a T-shaped bottom is simple, yet sturdy enough to stand up to plenty of traffic. It's also painted the same color as the trim elsewhere on the house, so it blends in.

Screen Door Styles

I F YOU LIKE THE LOOK of your front door and simply want the option of bringing in light during the winter and fresh breezes in summer, choose an all-purpose combination screen/storm door with a large open panel and no trim. (The screen and the glass panels are interchangeable, usually popping easily out of the frame.)

For something a little more traditional but still versatile, opt for the Colonial style, which looks appropriate on many types of homes.

The simple intersecting lines of the Arts and Crafts–style door would suit many types of early 20th century homes, or Neo-Arts and Crafts homes built more recently.

The same holds for Victorian and Neo-Victorian homes, which can benefit from a little gingerbread trim on the screen door frame.

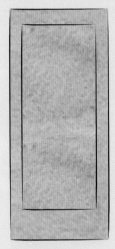
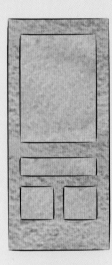
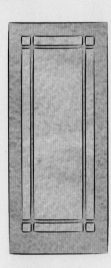
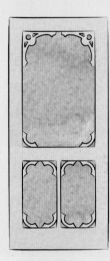

| All purpose | Colonial | Arts and Crafts | Victorian |

◀ A HOUSE WITH VICTORIAN ELEMENTS will benefit from a screen door with a bit of gingerbread—usually tucked into the corners of the frame or around the center divider. This door is painted a dark color that contrasts pleasantly with the white siding on the house.

▶ A SCREEN DOOR can add a little style—or a lot—to a front door. This version includes a picket fence-like kick panel at the bottom that echoes the shape and spacing of the nearby porch railings. Such similar details help to tie the overall entry together.

DOOR HARDWARE

▶ VICTORIAN DOOR SETS are known for their elaborate, flowing patterns. A vintage set can really set off an entry, and it's possible to find a complete set, from doorknobs to strike plates, from architectural salvage dealers. Or shop for a good-quality reproduction online or at a local home store.

▲ NOT ALL DOOR HANDLES are found at the local hardware store. Since most visitors are likely to notice the doorknob and handle on an entry, this is a good place to add an exceptional detail found at an antique or salvage store, like this unusual cast-metal dragon.

◀ SINCE MANY DOORS get worn and dirty around the doorknob, a large entry plate (a piece called an escutcheon) can add extra protection. If the escutcheon is copper, brass, or bronze, the plate may acquire the added benefit of a handsome patina.

▶ DOOR KNOCKERS are functional, but they can also make attractive door accents. A knocker doesn't have to match the entry hardware precisely—choose one made of the same metal or in a related style, or go for broke with a novelty piece in an interesting shape, like a dolphin, cluster of grapes, or palm tree.

▲ THIS MEDIEVAL-LOOKING DOOR gains a lot of style points from a pair of elaborate strap hinges. Although every door has hinges, these are largely for show. House numbers located directly beneath the lighting fixture ensure this house can be easily found morning, noon, or night.

▲ STRAP HINGES ARE A STRIKING and inexpensive way to dress up a door because they don't have to be functional. The hinges can either match or contrast with the door pulls. The strap hinges here are a key decorative element for this entry.

◀ DECORATIVE GRILLWORK is another form of hardware for the front door. While this example reflects the California Mission style of this 1920s home, it's adaptable to other types of doors. The grillwork can be kept locked when the door is open, providing ventilation and adding extra security.

◀ STYLE DETAILS on certain types of houses should be matched right down to the door hardware. Arts and Crafts homes are especially well known for their use of hammered copper and details like the square cutouts on this door plate.

IN THE DETAILS

Mailboxes

A MAILBOX is another important entry detail that can be easily personalized. While sturdy and serviceable mailboxes are available at the local home store, you can also cast a wider net and get something unique.

Look for antique or reproduction mailboxes from architectural salvage dealers and specialty stores, or use an unusual but stout container. If you have a deep, covered porch, for example, employ a sturdy basket for mail deliveries—just be sure to mount it securely. If you can find a mailbox that's made of brass, bronze, or copper, the metal will age and perhaps even gain an attractive patina.

▲ THIS VINTAGE MAILBOX is made out of black metal. The openwork owl decoration on the front serves a practical purpose, enabling the owner to see at a glance whether or not the day's mail has arrived.

▲ A LETTER SLOT is an attractive way to receive mail. The disadvantage is that the mail will fall through the slot onto your hall floor. To keep things tidy, install a basket or an open box under the slot indoors to catch magazines and letters.

LIGHTING

▲ AN UNUSUALLY ELEGANT rust-brown lantern mounted high over a door makes a striking accent light against a wall of light-colored stucco. Overhead illumination can be just as effective as light thrown off by fixtures located on either side of the door—it's simply a matter of personal taste.

▲ EXTERIOR SCONCE LIGHTS for entry doors can be mounted shallow to the wall or project dramatically, like this Arts and Crafts example. A projecting sconce is likely to throw more light, but take care to install it high enough that you won't bump your head.

▲ SCONCES—light fixtures that attach to a wall rather than a ceiling—are a good way to illuminate an entry, especially when they are used in pairs. Position fixtures where they will cast light on steps and the front door lock so you're able to enter your home safely.

▲ SOMETIMES THE MOST EFFECTIVE exterior lighting comes from within. The openwork porches on this shingle-style contemporary home allow lighting on exterior walls and under porch eaves to bounce outward, making the entire house a warm and welcoming presence.

◀ EXTERIOR LIGHTING doesn't have to be fancy to be effective. A simple metal pendant light installed close under the roof eave lights up this rustic doorstep and helps illuminate the nearby stone patio. Interior lights just inside the porch add extra ambiance.

◀ WHILE A WALL SCONCE IS useful for shedding a little light around an entry or passageway, consider the decorative possibilities offered by lanterns like this one. The cut-metal overlay of tree branches will cast interesting shadows against a wall or porch ceiling.

▲ FOR A RUSTIC LOOK that sheds plenty of light over a front door, consider a radial-wave lamp. Shielded by a flared metal shade and with the bulb protected by a cage, these industrial-strength lights stand up to outdoor use.

▲ LANTERNS DATE BACK to times when lanterns were carried by hand and then hung up outside a door to shed light. They are a good choice for traditional homes like this farmhouse.

◄ THE LIGHTING SCHEME on this home is as eclectic as the façade materials. Although three types of fixtures are used, they're far enough away from each other to make their own statement yet complement the exterior of the home.

► IF THE APPROACH to your entry climbs a flight of stairs, add small "wash" lights just above foot level every step or two. Visitors will easily be able to see the way up the stairs without light shining in their eyes.

FINISHING TOUCHES

▲ ▶ HOUSE NUMBERS are an inexpensive way to add real flair to a front door. Attractive ones are available in a variety of metals and finishes for just a few dollars apiece. Coordinate them to other elements on your home, such as the front doorknob or a door knocker.

◀ THINK OF A RAIN CHAIN as a cross between a decorative downspout and a wind chime. A rain chain breaks the fall of the water from your roof, guiding the water downward. The sound is similar to a bubbling fountain or flowing brook.

▲ IF YOU LIVE IN AN AREA that gets plenty of rainfall, consider adding a rain chain to channel water from your roof to a splashway or basin. Usually made of copper, rain chains can be shaped from linked chains, loops, inverted bells, or flower shapes.

▲ ALMOST ANY ELEMENT on your house can be decorative if you have enough imagination. These whimsical elephants made by a Vancouver coppersmith may not be to everyone's taste, but they are functional as well as artistic.

▲ ▼ A DOWNSPOUT can be a work of art in the right hands. Since a material like copper has to be cut and shaped to channel rainwater, it lends itself to decorative treatments like this thirsty fish.

▲ LITTLE DETAILS make a big difference around the front door. Even an element as small as a door buzzer can add a pinch of punch. Home stores and online suppliers offer dozens of styles, from a traditional fleur-de-lis to a contemporary bull's-eye.

▲ A DOOR KNOCKER not only makes a satisfying thunk when guests come calling but it also can be a signature statement for your door. Traditional door knockers include hefty loops that you grasp in one hand. The knocker either taps directly against the door or against a dedicated plate.

Landings and Porches

EVERY ENTRY MUST HAVE AN APPROACH—a series of elements that create a smooth transition to your front door. Landings (or stoops) and porches fall into this category because they provide a resting place to gather the mail or get out the front door key.

The most simple landing can be a single stone step or fan of concrete before the front door. More elaborate examples include flights of steps leading to a landing, small decks, porches just large enough to protect the entry from inclement weather, and large porches that span the entire front of a house.

The more room for a landing, the more fun you can have with it. Some landings are big enough to furnish like an outdoor room, while others are tiny, with just enough space for a small accent, like an antique boot scraper.

▲ IF SPACE PERMITS, a landing should have a bench or, at the very least, a small chair. This deck is just wide enough for a cozy bench with pillows and an old metal dairy sign as a backdrop. A potted evergreen and a wind chime make this an inviting place to linger.

▶ A REAL VICTORIAN PORCH makes an ideal outdoor living room. This gingerbread-trimmed example is painted in festive colors and furnished with rocking chairs and a wicker planter. Pots of hanging impatiens pick up colors in the trim.

▲ THIS LANDING in the corner of a broad porch is essentially transformed into an outdoor room, providing a comfortable resting spot for guests and visitors as well as an inviting space for homeowners to enjoy the outdoors. Cozy details include a rustic settee and chair, a side table, and shade-loving plants.

STEPS AND STOOPS

▲ SURROUNDED BY LOW FLOWERING shrubs and grasses, a few steps lead to a landing on an old stone house. The open landing, made of material the same color as the house, helps draw attention to the beautiful old façade.

▲ THIS ENTRY IS ENHANCED by a landing with interesting patterns. The outer bricks are turned on their sides, facing outward from the front door, while a diamond pattern is displayed on the inner part of the tread. Additional patterns are found in the railing, the door, and even the lantern.

▲ SOME FLORAL ACCENTS can be spontaneous, like this burst of bright purple ground cover growing right through the treads of a series of wide wood steps. Steps made of durable woods like cedar and mahogany make sense in temperate climates where freezing and thawing aren't much of an issue.

◄ THIS LANDING can be approached from two sides— an advantage given that the steps are open and unprotected, and that there is no handrail. The design is simple yet elegant— the steps seem to float as they rise up to the door.

◄ STEPS SHOULD BE CUT to a comfortable height for ease of use. Hard stones like granite make excellent choices in harsh, wintry climates because they don't crack or erode easily. Runs should be kept short; long flights of stone steps can be hazardous in wet or icy weather.

Stair Railings

STAIR RAILINGS ARE ESSENTIAL FOR entry staircases with three or more steps. While you can make do with a sturdy metal handrail or a stock railing from a builder's-supply or home store, the entry will look better if the railing is tailored to the rest of the trim on your house. There are companies that specialize in custom metal and wood railings, and you might be able to find a local artisan in your own community who can make your design.

A simple railing consists of a diagonal run of straight spindles held in place by top and bottom rails, affixed to posts at the top and the bottom of the stair. You can elaborate on the basic form by adding extra shaping or decorative millwork to any of the components.

If the railing will be made of wood, choose a durable, long-lived species like mahogany, and keep the wood sealed or painted to protect it from rot.

▲ AN ENTRY AT THE TOP of a long flight of stairs is an opportunity to add a decorative porch railing. In this case where the entry landing is raised over the garage, the railing is made up of narrowly spaced boards enhanced with cutwork diamonds.

▶ STAIR RAILINGS should reflect the style of the house. These massive posts and stout porch railings complement other architectural millwork on a high-style Victorian home. The steps, of poured concrete, are almost incidental to the design.

▶ WHENEVER THERE ARE TWO or more steps, it's a good idea to add at least one hand rail—preferably two—for safety. This Folk Victorian home has a rail on either side of the steps, making it easy for two people to reach the landing at a time.

◀ STEPS FACED WITH STONES suggest a rocky coastal environment. While stone is a traditional material for steps and stoops in New England and the mid-Atlantic, the use here is more decorative, with the stones embedded in concrete or cement.

COVERED ENTRIES

▶ A COVERED ENTRY can make a real statement on a house. This one gets its sense of presence from grouped pillars supporting a massive porch roof with a temple-like gable. Integral benches with stylish cutouts add a welcoming air.

▼ LOCATING A PERGOLA near an entry porch is a good option in a dry, sunny climate, where frequent downpours are not a problem. Plant climbing vines near the wood posts, and ultimately you will have a shade-covered sitting area.

▶ THERE IS NO better argument for a covered entry than snowy weather. If you live in a climate where the snow level can easily reach the porch landing, some kind of protection is a must.

▼ THIS COLUMNED PORCH projects well out from the front of the house, covering not only the entry but also the windows on either side. The style is a favorite in the South, where abundant light makes shade something to be desired.

▲ A COVERED ENTRY that is integrated into the roofline can be an elegant piece of architecture. This one, supported by a simple tapered column, is covered by a shallow, undulating roof form known as an "eyebrow" curve.

Covering an Entry

NOTHING CREATES CURB APPEAL as quickly as a well-designed entry porch. Surprisingly, entry porches are far down the wish list of most-desired remodeling projects. Yet a welcoming entry porch almost automatically makes a house more appealing to guests or would-be buyers.

The simplest covered entry is one that protects only the front stoop. The roof can be a peaked gable (a and c) or a pitched shed style (b). (A gable roof has the extra advantage of diverting rain down the sides rather than the front like a shed roof.)

Even more desirable is a full front porch, extending across the full width of the house (d). A full porch creates extra usable space and makes the house appear much larger than it actually is.

a

c

b

d

▶ LOW LANDINGS often lack architectural presence. This one gets added punch from a projecting, arched canopy and dramatically splayed pillars. The dark tropical wood on the landing and stair steps is not only durable, but it contrasts well with the white trim.

WHEN A FRONT YARD is private, the approach to the entry can be almost as relaxed as a backyard patio. Here, low stone walls enclose a small courtyard, where there is enough space for a dining area and a bench under the porch.

▼ THE BIGGER THE PORCH, the more it becomes an extension of the house, literally adding square footage to the overall space of your home. This long, wide veranda is furnished with two sitting areas, including one with a table for dining or playing cards or board games.

◄ THE COVERED ENTRY on this recently remodeled Cape-style home plays off other architectural shapes on the house, notably the end gable and the dormer gables on the second story. The bumped-out rooflines give the house architectural relief, but the overall effect is harmonious.

PORCHES

▼ A COTTAGE-STYLE ENTRY set back on a deep porch is open and welcoming. To bring extra light into the house, the owner opted to install glass panes in and around the door, including the narrow side windows called sidelights.

CHANGING THE ROOFLINE of the porch from a low flat extension to a wide, dramatic gable transformed the look of this home. Although the house is technically no bigger, it appears much more substantial thanks to the new peaked roof.

THE ENTRY PORCH on this single-story Cape-style home extends across most of the front of the house, but the flat roof makes it look cramped and unappealing. The owners decided to rethink its shape as part of a cosmetic makeover.

A COVERED PORCH can be useful on the side of the house, especially if there are entrances to guest quarters along the passage. Lighting should be spaced every few feet to ensure the entire length of the structure is well-lit.

▼ A PORCH THAT GETS several hours of sunlight daily is an ideal place to grow flowers. For best effect, place plants at different heights—low to the ground, at the windowsill, and hanging just beneath the porch roof—to create a cascade of foliage and blossoms.

▲ A PAIR OF CANE-BACK ROCKING CHAIRS adds instant appeal to any porch. Porches are also good places to display large pieces of pottery, often called jardinières. They can hold plants or simply be decorative, like this oversized example.

▲ WITH A BANK OF WINDOWS with paneled shutters as a backdrop, the owner of this attractive space has created a relaxing outdoor living room on the porch. Various pieces of wicker form a casual seating area around an indoor–outdoor rug.

▲ FULL-WIDTH PORCHES are a charming throwback to the past, and make a house seem more expansive. Think of the posts that support the porch roof as a decorating opportunity: Use columns or shaped posts, like the ones on this Neo-Victorian house.

◄ YOU CAN ADD CHARM to a porch with surprisingly few details. The accents here include a screen door painted red, a single painted rocker, and a fringe of gingerbread along the edge of the porch ceiling.

The Approach

The path to your front door should be a journey of small pleasures that appeals to the senses. Just think of neatly cropped grass bordering a meandering stone walkway, the scent of blooming roses in well-tended planting beds, or the rustle of leaves from a nearby stand of trees. Such sights, smells, and sounds will leave a good and lasting impression to visitors and passersby.

Even if your yard is the standard-issue rectangle of grass with shrubbery hugging the foundation of the house, try to envision it as a landscape that you can shape. Begin by assessing your site and looking for ways to enhance it. Is the grass healthy and green? Are the plants in the yard about the right size and scale or are they overgrown or nonexistent? Is there an attractive path that leads guests to the front door?

Consider both the limitations and possibilities of your front yard, and select materials and plants that best suit the climate and your degree of interest in gardening and lawn maintenance. The key elements to consider for maximum impact are landscaping plants (including grass, flowers, ground covers, shrubbery, and trees), paths and walkways, and one aspect you might have overlooked—outdoor lighting.

◄ THIS HOUSE ALREADY HAS STORYBOOK APPEAL, but the landscape sets the stage for it. A brick path winds its way to the front door through a well-kept lawn and lush beds of flowering plants and ornamental trees.

Shaping the Landscape

THERE ARE AN INFINITE NUMBER OF WAYS to shape and define your home landscape. While an expanse of healthy grass can make a front yard appealing, so can a terraced hill landscaped with stones, retaining walls, and shrubbery, or a "dry" front yard with drought-resistant plants and beds of stone or rock.

Begin by evaluating your site. Is the grass in good shape? Are the foundation plants ragged? Next, think about what you'd like your front yard to become. Should you add shade trees, beds of flowers, or a new pathway? Some approaches require a lot of maintenance, but that's not a problem if you can afford regular landscape care or if you're ready to do the work yourself.

▲ GRASS CAN MAKE A LOVELY front landscape, particularly if your house is painted white. Keep the lawn mowed regularly, and remove the clippings when you cut so that thatch doesn't build up and smother new growth.

◄ A CURVING BRICK PATH trimmed with stone not only creates a clear passage to the front of this house but also gives shape and definition to planting beds on either side of the passage. A bonus: There's little grass to cut.

▲ THIS FRONT YARD is particularly welcoming due to the charming flower garden enclosed by a white picket fence. Visitors enter the garden by stepping in between peaked-roof posts that double as tiny birdhouses.

Assessing Your Site

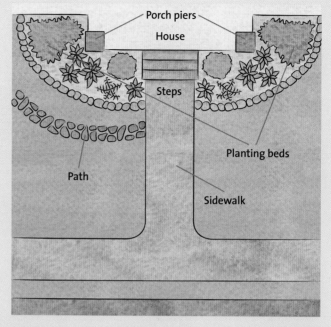

BEFORE YOU BEGIN re-creating your front yard, get out some graph paper and a 25-ft. measuring tape and create a site plan. Draw a sketch of the property boundaries and the placement of the house roughly to scale (measure widths and distances between the house and other features like the driveway and large trees). Then locate the key landscaping elements in your yard on the sketch.

Stand at the edge of the yard with the sketch in hand. What's missing? What needs to be replaced? Should you add an ornamental tree surrounded by flower beds on one side of the yard, or replace a concrete path with a brick one?

Consider the results from a three-dimensional perspective; the most pleasant yards include landscaping elements that vary in height and texture.

▲ A BUNGALOW PORCH IS TRIMMED with neat circular planting beds that seem to flow around the massive stone pillars supporting the roof. The vegetation not only softens the line between the house and the yard but also extends the welcome out into the yard.

ONE OF THE MOST EFFECTIVE WAYS to use foundation shrubs is to plant them in successive tiers, with shorter shrubs in front of taller ones. This technique creates visual interest, allowing you to see a variety of foliage at different levels. Here, evergreens make a pleasing backdrop for banks of flowering hydrangeas.

PORCHES ARE transitional spaces that should be welcoming and restful—characteristics that should be apparent whether you're coming from inside the house or from the front yard. Here, a pair of comfortable and colorful Adirondack chairs invites visitors to linger.

ANOTHER ATTRACTIVE WAY to incorporate a covered entry is to recess it underneath second-story living space. This one on the corner of a house with a steeply pitched roof is easily accessible to the driveway, front yard, and side patio, thanks to broad steps that wrap around the landing.

▲ IF YOUR YARD is especially spacious, edge a walk with a deep bed of plants that vary in height, color, size, and texture. Position low ground covers nearest the path, with plants that will create the most spectacular show in the middle or rear of the bed.

▶ POTTED BOXWOOD TOPIARIES and a leafy climbing clematis soften a small brick courtyard leading to a formal front door. Without the plantings to break up the many hard surfaces, the approach would seem cold and stark.

Using Plants Effectively

Follow these guidelines to create a front yard with appealing landscaping.

- Choose plants that are easy to grow and maintain.

- Make sure your plants suit both the soil and the amount of light the yard receives. In many states, you can have the soil tested by a local agricultural agent for factors like alkalinity and nitrogen content. If the yard is sunny, you'll be able to choose from a wide variety of plants and flowers; if it's shady, you'll need to look for shade-loving varieties.

- Create visual interest and vary textures by "layering" plants. Put the tallest specimens at the back and the lowest in the front.

- Choose plants that offer a lot of variation in foliage and range of color (light and variegated greens to deep glossy greens).

- Look for species that offer changes from season to season. Boston ivy, for example, offers green foliage in spring, berries in summer, red foliage in fall, and interesting vine patterns in winter.

▲ THE PATH TO THE FRONT DOOR can be attractive without being a blank slate of newly mown grass. Low, brushy ground cover, flowering shrubs, and a climbing vine with dark, glossy leaves make a soft, inviting frame for this doorway.

◄ THIS HOME USES the hillside landscape to create a welcoming trip to the front door. A walkway of mixed materials creates visual interest and the landings between the steps allow guests to enjoy the native plantings.

FLOWERS AND FOLIAGE

▲ WINDOW BOXES ARE A GREAT WAY to soften the line between your house and the front landscape. Window-box plantings, which can be changed seasonally, provide a bright burst of accent color to the front of your house.

▲ FLOWERS AREN'T THE ONLY WAY to add color to your landscape. Mixing plants with leaves of different colors and textures is one of the best ways to keep your landscape interesting all year, especially if the plants are massed for a graduated effect.

▶ EVEN IF THE "LAWN" IS COVERED with a visually appealing pattern of brick, you can still create a diverse landscape with potted plants that vary in terms of leaf shapes, sizes, flowers, and colors. Be sure to add some seating, too, so visitors can pause to enjoy the display.

▲ INCORPORATE WALLS and other
hardscape features as part of
a plan to edge or layer plants for
dramatic effect. A bed of flowering purple flowers explodes with
color against a low stone wall of
flat, beige boulders.

◄ TWO DIFFERENT VARIETIES of
hydrangea—one purplish blue,
the other white—are massed
against each other to create a
stunning summer display. To
maintain visual interest at other
times of the year, mix in ornamental shrubs that shine in
other seasons, such as pyracan-
tha or holly.

The Approach 109

▶ A LOW ADOBE-RED WALL
and brilliant desert flowers and cactus highlight the approach to a Spanish Colonial style house in Arizona. Incorporating plant species that are native to your area will usually reward you with ease of care and bursts of color in spring and summer.

Adding a Fountain

WATER FEATURES tend to have a soothing effect—a good reason to add one if your intention is to make your yard a relaxing retreat.

Small fountains are often sold with all the parts you need to set them up. A fountain kit consists of a basin to hold the water and a decorative spout or vessel that conceals the tube that funnels water into the basin. A small internal pump shoots the water through the fountain; in most cases, the water recirculates. You only need to refill the basin as water evaporates. Most fountains run on electricity, so you'll either need to have a power outlet close at hand or be prepared to dig a trench for a grounded line.

Fountains can be made of almost any material, including stone, concrete, and metals like copper and steel. They also can be highly decorative—almost like a sculpture.

▶ THE SOFT, GURGLING SOUNDS of moving water has a soothing effect. That explains why fountains appeal to the senses. Here, water streams from an old tin watering can-turned-fountain into a waiting basin. Even a small fountain helps circulate air and adds moisture to a garden.

▲ A SMALL FRONT YARD is a great place to experiment with flowering plants and grasses. Allow ample room for a pathway like this jagged flagstone walk, and choose flowering species, grasses, and ground covers geared toward the amount of light the area receives, whether sunny or shady.

◄ COTTAGE-STYLE GARDENS are often a riot of overgrown plants and flowers with no grass in sight. This one maintains a bit of order, however, thanks to a wood fence and a wide gate topped with a pergola.

Color Combinations

CREATING GREAT-LOOKING PLANT combinations is easier said than done. While it might seem logical to use two flowers of the same color together, for instance, they might not actually complement each other if one is a hot version of that color and one is cool. Have fun planting flowers together but realize that it might take some trial and error to get just the right combination. Here are some ideas to get you started.

▲ New Guinea impatiens, caladium, and green dragon aroid.

▲ Globe amaranth, tropical smoke bush, and flowering tobacco.

▲ Mealycup sage, zinnia, and coneflower.

▲ Purple shamrock, ornamental pepper, impatiens, and heliotrope.

▲ Pacific hybrid delphiniums, Asiatic lily, and ligularia.

▲ CREATE A SHOW OF COLOR with blooming plants that come in an array of pastels, like impatiens, petunias, or azaleas. Group them in single-color beds, or mix and match colors to create beds with high contrast (i.e., red and white) or graduated colors (white, pink, and fuchsia, for example).

◀ EVEN WHEN YOUR HOME is a row house right on the street and sidewalk, there is always room for flowers. A long built-in planter under a bank of windows on the third floor provides a show of color all summer long.

▶ EVEN IF CERTAIN PLANTS
grow like weeds in your area,
they can still be successfully
used for landscaping as
accents at the edge of a
lawn or displayed in planters.
The approach to this enclosed
courtyard entry in a sub-
tropical location makes good
use of native palmetto and
saw grass.

◀ IT'S POSSIBLE TO CREATE
an attractive front yard without
any grass at all. A low, branching
evergreen surrounded by a bed
of pebbles is the focal point here;
other beds of larger stones and
paved stone walks add diversity
of texture.

Rock Gardens

A ROCK GARDEN IS A SCULPTURED LANDSCAPE that uses rocks, boulders, and small and large stones along with soil and plants to create the appearance of a natural landscape. It can have paths, beds of plants, shrubs, even rock terraces and trees.

Whether natural to your landscape or purchased from a landscaping-supply store, rock should be used to create focal points, set off plantings, and hold the soil in place. You may also need to add soil to your lot if the existing soil is thin or poor.

Certain plants thrive in rocky conditions. To find out which plants grow best in your climate, consult your local nursery.

▶ IN A YARD STREWN WITH BOULDERS and flat embedded rock, nature gets a little help from a few scattered planting beds and terraced planters made of stacked stone. The contrast between soil, greenery, and rock gives this garden an austere beauty.

◀ WATER FEATURES CAN ADD a sense of peace and calm to a landscape. Here, a private lake creates a stunning foreground for this contemporary house with large expanses of glass. At night, indoor light throws reflections on the water, intensifying the dramatic effect.

Xeriscaping

IF YOU LIVE IN A CLIMATE where water is scarce and expensive, consider xeriscaping, a type of front yard garden that minimizes water use. (The word—coined about 25 years ago—comes from the Greek word for "dry" plus landscaping.)

A xeriscape isn't necessarily a grass- and plant-free zone. Instead, a xeriscape incorporates flowering plants, shrubs, and trees that are water efficient and uses them as focal points for a lawn that is largely covered with other natural features, such as large rocks, pebbled paths, and mulch. Plants with similar water needs are often grouped together to create the feel of an oasis in the desert.

Xeriscapes work, too: A properly maintained xeriscape uses less than half the water of a traditional lawn-based yard.

▲ A XERISCAPE ISN'T THE SAME as a "zero-scape" which uses no plants at all except for a few desert species. This lawn manages to look lush and interesting with a handful of ornamental trees, shrubbery, beds of mulch, and a flowing path of pebbles.

◀ DETAILS CAN MAKE all the difference. This ring of flat, narrow stones laid in a starburst pattern makes an attractive accent around a white-barked birch tree. The stones almost seem to point to the display of nearby tulips.

▼ A DRY STONE BED BORDERING a more traditional planting bed includes several sizes and colors of stone. Striking and attractive in its own right, it also helps keep moisture where it's most needed and helps prevent erosion.

◀ ENCLOSED FRONT GARDENS DATE back to Colonial times when roving livestock made it a necessity to fence in flowers. This private garden, accessed through arched gates on either side, has a sense of secrecy that makes discovering its gravel paths and flowering species a delight for visitors and guests.

A Terrace Makeover

A STEEP FRONT YARD makes special demands on a homeowner. Terracing and plants must hold the soil in place, but neither element should overwhelm the other—or the appearance of the house itself. Ideally, the path from street to front door should be easy to negotiate and pleasing in appearance.

▲ THE NEW, WIDER STAIRS include a small landing after the first four steps—a chance to catch your breath on the way up. The light-colored stone and concrete terrace walls seem to open up the space, making the small hillside appear larger than it actually is.

▼ THE NEW PLAN completely transforms both landscape and house. Rather than a large single bed of green, the planting beds include species of varied shapes, textures, and colors. The different colors complement the new, warmer shade on the house.

▲ THE OLD STAIRS CLIMB directly up from the street, without a pause. The brick retaining wall shows evidence of cracking and discoloration, and a row of stones intrudes between the steps and a planting bed that could use a ground cover.

▲ ON THIS TERRACED LOT, the planting beds are not only overgrown, but they are dull and featureless, doing little to enhance the white stucco and brick house.

 ▲ A STONE WALL neatly divides the approach to this contemporary farmhouse into upper and lower yards. A set of stone steps angles left into the upper yard, while a flight of wooden steps doglegs right to the front door, creating an interesting tension.

▶ THE PLANTS IN THIS FRONT-YARD cottage garden reflect the style of the house. They are enclosed by a picket fence painted to match the house trim and offer a wash of color to an otherwise subdued color palette.

Walks and Paths

THE PATH TO YOUR FRONT DOOR may cover a small amount of ground, but it has a big impact on the overall appeal of your yard. Like the entry, a front walk should be a focal point—functional, easy to see, and a pleasure to use. While there's nothing wrong with a path that marches straight through the yard to the entry, front walks can also bend or zigzag with the terrain or gently curve through or around other features in the yard, such as flower beds or stands of trees.

Almost any material that drains well and stands up to the weather can make a good front walkway, including gravel, concrete, brick, and stone. Although the surface should provide good footing in all kinds of weather (especially when it's icy or wet), it should have visual interest, too.

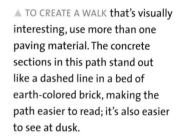

▲ TO CREATE A WALK that's visually interesting, use more than one paving material. The concrete sections in this path stand out like a dashed line in a bed of earth-colored brick, making the path easier to read; it's also easier to see at dusk.

◄ STONE LAID IN A formal pattern makes a beeline to a guest house across this patch of smooth lawn. The side path is far less formal: The two irregularly shaped stones suggest stepping stones in a "pond" of grass.

◄ A BRICK PATH adds a sense of order to a riot of roses, flowering shrubs, and ground cover in this cottage-style garden. Brick lasts a long time, has an interesting texture, and its variable coloring makes a pleasing contrast for growing plants.

▼ THIS STONE PATH makes its way through a hillside garden. To create a walkway on a slope requires minor excavation: You'll need to level the soil for the steps as the hill gradually rises. Plant a year-round ground cover such as pachysandra or creeping myrtle on either side of the steps to minimize erosion.

◀ IF YOUR YARD has a sharp drop or a creek running through it, a raised walkway is one method of keeping the path to the front door relatively flat and dry. This one, made of weather-resistant decking material, includes lighting along the railing for a safe approach at night.

▲ FORMAL ENTRIES are often symmetrical. This house with its central entry and windows balanced on either side calls out for a front path that's centered on the front door. Even the bricks themselves emphasize the formal design: They are laid so that they line up with the entry.

▶ CONCRETE WALKS can be dressed up or disguised in any number of ways. This walk features a pattern of cracks that makes it look like flagstone. Although today's concrete can be tinted or made to look like stone, it's easier to create a new look when the material is freshly mixed and laid.

◀ NATURAL STONE PAVERS in a repeating pattern follow a curving path from a trellised arbor to the front porch. The surface of the pavers has a lot of texture, which makes them easier to walk on when the ground is wet or icy.

▼ THIS TINY BEACH COTTAGE in town uses the sidewalk to welcome guests to the front door. Colorful, spreading plants break through the hard lines of the fence.

BRICK

◄ COMBINING DIFFERENT PATTERNS
and colors of brick can add a lot of
interest to a path. This walk, which
creates a cul de sac with a tree as
its focal point, incorporates several
shades of brick and two kinds
of edging.

▼ ALLOW A GENEROUS AMOUNT
of room for planting beds or grass
between your home and any
path that parallels it. Here, dense
foliage softens the transition
between the brick walk, laid
in a herringbone pattern, and
the house.

▲ BRICK WALKS ALMOST ALWAYS
have borders to give them a crisp
edge. This series of intersecting
walks in a running bond pattern is
trimmed with the most common
edging pattern—a straight line of
bricks laid perpendicular to the
main run of the walk.

Brick Walks

THERE ARE HUNDREDS OF VARIATIONS of brick patterns for walks. Some of the most common are running bond, basket weave, herringbone, and diagonal. Any of these patterns, properly laid, will reward you with an attractive, durable path for years to come.

Laying a brick walk can be hard work, but it isn't hard to do. Begin by excavating a bed at least 4 in. deeper than the depth of the pavers you intend to use. Fill the bed with a 4-in. layer of stone dust. Tamp the dust down and mist it with water. Then begin laying your pavers, beginning with the border. (Use hard-fired paving brick—not old bricks left over from a construction site—or parts of your walk may begin to crack or crumble after a few seasons.) Pack the bricks in tightly, and tamp down with a mallet.

To trim a brick to fit, use a brick set, a broad-bladed masonry chisel, and the mallet. When you need to make a cut, draw a line across the edge of the brick where you want to remove excess material. Hold the edge of the brick set firmly on the line with the beveled side away from the part of the brick you intend to use. Strike the tool firmly with the mallet, and it should break cleanly.

Once the pattern is laid, fill in the cracks with more stone dust to prevent grass from gaining a foothold, then mist with a hose to set it. (You may want to repeat this process once the dust has had time to settle.)

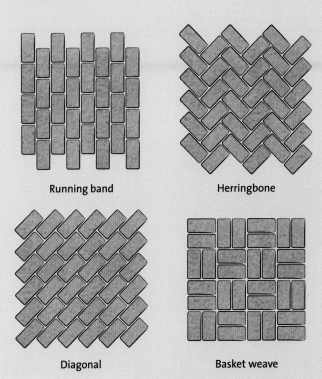

Running band

Herringbone

Diagonal

Basket weave

▲ AN ATTRACTIVE PAVED AREA like this driveway set with brick pavers can lead naturally into a front walkway. Creating one continuous surface also helps establish and define planting areas for a show of seasonal color.

▲ THIS PATH IS ACTUALLY A SERIES of stepping stones with a novel twist. These footsteps are composed of multiple bricks in a herringbone pattern. Although the effect is traditional, the path is anything but ordinary.

STONE

▶ A COVERED WALK THAT SETS OFF a raked Japanese garden is paved with cut pieces of thin, evenly layered stone called flagstone. Although flagstone makes an elegant and durable walk, the material tends to be expensive. A more affordable alternative is concrete that's made to look like stone.

▲ THIS RAMBLING PATH makes use of locally available stones such as granite and irregularly shaped flagstone. To keep grass from creeping in, fill in cracks and crevices between larger stones with crushed rock or chipped gravel, or plant a fragrant, low-growing ground cover such as creeping thyme.

▶ BRICK, STONE, AND GRAVEL aren't the only materials for paths and walkways. If your budget allows, add drama with unusual materials and textures. Here, a side path of rubbed stones leads to a formal walk of tile in a checkerboard pattern.

▲ HARD, ALMOST IMPENETRABLE
stones like granite will serve long
and well as steps cut into the side
of a hill, even in a harsh climate.
This retaining wall is dry-stacked,
meaning each stone is laid in
place by hand without mortar,
creating a more natural look
for the wall.

▶ SQUARE, BLOCKY PAVERS set in
mortar are laid with free-form
edges in this garden path. The
unusual edge treatment and the
irregular path of the walk suggest
a rocky river overflowing its
banks, a nice touch in a garden
without grass or lush plantings.

STONE PAVERS work well with other materials: In this Asian-inspired courtyard, the pavers combine with a wide boardwalk to create a serene mood. Laying the boards perpendicular to the pavers allows the texture of both materials to stand out.

▼ **BECAUSE CUT FLAGSTONE** is available in squares and rectangles of different sizes, it lends itself to interesting patterns for walks and paths. This composition gets an extra jolt of color from the use of brick squares as accents.

▶ **A PATH OF LIGHT-COLORED** flagstone meanders through this colorful summer flower garden. The gaps between the stones have been allowed to fill in with a low, creeping ground cover, which adds extra texture and contrast to the path.

▲ LARGE PIECES OF FLAGSTONE make a wide, enduring divider between stands of grasses and flowers, both of which help to soften the sharp edges of the stone. Cut stone is one of the most expensive materials for walkways, but it lasts far longer and needs less care than gravel or mulch.

▼ A SHORT FLIGHT OF STONE STEPS centered on the front door of a Colonial-era house abruptly ends when it reaches the lawn, suggesting that its original purpose—as a stop for carriages— is long gone. Now it's just an intriguing feature that draws the eye to the front door.

Lighting the Landscape

W HILE IT'S IMPORTANT to light paths, steps, doorways, and driveways for visibility and safety reasons, lighting can also enhance your home's curb appeal by adding a sense of drama, especially at night.

Choose outdoor fixtures that direct light either up, down, or to one side. Uplights in or near the ground make sense when you want to accent a tree or cast light on the front of the house. Downlights are an alternative if you want to illuminate a path from above or spotlight a side yard with lighting recessed into an eave.

Unless the light fixture is especially attractive, try to conceal or minimize it. You want to emphasize the stone path or that lovely specimen tree, not the high-tech-looking fixture mounted on a post or staked in the ground. Used skillfully, outdoor lighting can make your home safe and beautiful.

▲ FOOTLIGHTS RECESSED into low stone walls that flank nearby steps are a great safety feature in snowy climates. These fixtures cast light directly on the steps, while a pair of hanging down-lights illuminates the landing.

◀ LARGE LANTERNS on either side of this doorway cast warm ambient light, but they don't do much to illuminate the large covered entryway. They get some help, however, from a concealed light mounted on one of the beams that span the entry roof.

▲ CONCEALED DOWNLIGHTS give a big boost to a pendant light in the entry of this rustic fishing lodge. While the entry light is large and attractive, most of the illumination actually comes from lights recessed in the eaves and porch ceiling.

▲ LIGHTED POSTS, which cast illumination sideways and downward, are an effective way to light the passage into a driveway or parking area. These attractive lanterns are mounted on low tapered piers finished with shingles that complement the shingle siding on the garage and the main house.

LIGHTING PATHS AND WALKWAYS

◄ A COLONIAL-STYLE post lantern is well suited to this mid-20th-century house in the same style. While the single post light casts enough illumination for a relatively short path, a longer walkway would require a series of fixtures so that the pools of light overlap and illuminate the entire length of the walk.

► UNLESS THEY'RE especially handsome, exterior light fixtures should not be visible in the daytime. This lamp on the entry wall is the only fixture with a lot of visibility in a yard filled with small, discreet lights. At night, the lantern "calls out" the stone wall and illuminates its interesting texture.

▲ A LIGHT CAN SERVE more than one purpose, particularly if it's attractive. This Japanese-inspired wood-and-copper lantern not only highlights the turn-in for a driveway, but also it makes a nice focal point for a low stone wall.

▲ A RAISED WALKWAY gets plenty of illumination from small sconces mounted at foot level. The tiny footlights, which are fairly easy to install, make an evening passage along the walk a safe and pleasant experience.

Low-Voltage Lighting Systems

LOW-VOLTAGE LIGHTS are a great way to put light right where you want it in your yard. Use them to illuminate paths, steps, and walkways as accent lighting or for low-level general illumination. The fixtures run off a transformer that plugs into a standard wall outlet, ramping down the standard 120-volt energy flow to a mere 12 volts.

The small, compact lights are linked together by 12-gauge wire cable, which runs along the ground. It's a good idea to make sure the cable is placed in areas where it isn't likely to be disturbed, such as under shrubs or along fences. The lights can be mounted on posts, staked in the ground, or concealed in shrubbery or planting beds.

Like other forms of exterior lighting, low-voltage lights can point up or down to draw attention to a specimen tree or a special feature of your home, like a fountain. You can also use them as backlights to create a silhouette effect. Despite their low voltage, these lights are exceptionally bright, so make sure you use them sparingly to target specific features.

The lights can be activated by a number of means, including timers and photoelectric cells that generate light after dark. While the components for a low-voltage system are relatively inexpensive (a small kit costs only a few hundred dollars), it's best to have your outdoor lighting installed by a landscaping professional experienced with these kinds of systems.

▲ LOW-VOLTAGE LIGHTING installed along the path to a front door provides illumination for nighttime visitors. The up-facing lights also cast dramatic accent lighting on both the entry and the crape myrtle trees that line the walk.

▲ HARDWIRED EXTERIOR LIGHTING must be installed by an electrician and meet local electrical codes, usually making it a more expensive choice than low-voltage lighting. But hardwiring is a must for lights at the end of a long run from the power source, such as this driveway fixture.

▲ THE LONG ENTRY CORRIDOR for this factory-built house is illuminated with sconces mounted high on the wall, just under the porch roof. Although wall-mounted fixtures work just as well as lights mounted in the eaves, they should be attractive, since they'll be visible day and night.

◄ WHENEVER A WALKWAY intersects with an element like a stone wall, it's a good idea to add lighting for safety reasons. The light not only keeps visitors from bumping into the wall, but it also helps define the transition from a more public space into a more private one.

Supporting Players

You've mulled over the design possibilities of the front of the house—the entry, the lawn, and the lighting. But have you given any thought to supporting structures like gates and garages, fences and driveways? All of these elements are large and prominent features that can make or break the overall appearance of your home.

Fences and gates are important for privacy and security reasons, but because they cover so much of the landscape, it's essential that they be attractive as well as secure. To make a fence more of a handsome feature, consider adding highly decorative garden structures like arbors and pergolas.

Driveways and garages are often a given: For better or worse, they come with the house. But a garage or driveway can undergo a makeover as easily as any other part of your home or yard. Any garage will look better if the details on or around the door harmonize with exterior elements elsewhere on the house. And a driveway can be completely transformed just by upgrading paving materials.

◄ THIS GRAND ENTRANCE enclosed by a gated stone wall makes use of three of the most common materials for driveways—asphalt, stone pavers, and gravel. Stone pavers are an attractive feature and they serve a practical purpose: They keep gravel from washing out onto the asphalt.

Fences, Walls, and Gates

FENCES AND WALLS serve many purposes. They define property lines, create privacy, keep wandering animals in or out, even shore up a terrace or a sloped yard. But from the standpoint of curb appeal, they should always be attractive as well as functional.

Materials for fences include wood, vinyl, and metal. The most durable and attractive woods for fences include cedar and redwood. But no matter which material you choose, keep in mind that in a front yard, a fence should be "friendly." That means you want it to be open enough to see through. Place the gate so that it allows for easy passage into the front yard; in most cases, it should open onto the path to the front door.

Walls are usually made of stone or brick. These sturdy constructions suggest a degree of substance and permanence in addition to their other roles. To keep a stone or brick wall neighborly, make sure it's not much taller than waist high.

▲ A GATE DOESN'T necessarily need to match its fence to be charming. This substantial double-door gate in natural wood resembles a double entry door. The Arts-and-Crafts–style "windows" in each panel make the doors seem friendly and approachable to guests and visitors.

◄ NOTHING SETS OFF A LANDSCAPE like a stone wall. Because each stone is laid individually, a stone wall can be tailored to fit any yard. Unlike mortared stone walls, drystacked stone walls have a natural appearance. Because they require masonry skills to carefully set each stone without mortar, however, they tend to be costly.

A WHITE PICKET FENCE is the perfect enclosure for older or more traditional homes. This fence clearly outlines property borders, but it's also charming and easy to see through. It also features an unusual turnstile gate. To add a splash of color, plant climbing roses or clematis at the base of the arbor posts.

PLANK FENCING is an attractive solution for an area where you want privacy. Usually made of cedar, plank fences are built in ready-made sections that attach to pressure-treated posts dug on site. In this fence, the top sections include latticework to allow some light and visibility into the yard.

FENCES AND GATES

▲ EVEN IF ITS DESIGN allows visitors to peak inside, a fence can still provide privacy. Although this gray and white fence is composed of wide and narrow slats with narrow gaps between them, it's difficult to see inside without making an effort.

▶ IN THE RIGHT SETTING, a simple post fence and gate can look just right. This airy post-and-rail fence is made of inexpensive and easily available cedar. Its open style defines the property line without interfering with the spectacular view.

▶ THE CENTERPIECE of any fence is the front gate. The posts on either side of the gate should be a little larger than those on the rest of the fence so that the gate stands out. To call even more attention to the gate, add decorative elements to the posts like these ball finials.

▲ A PLANK GATE gives even the flimsiest fence a sense of substance. Hanging lanterns on either side of this scalloped-shape gate with a delightful overhead arbor ensure a safe and warm welcome well after the sun goes down.

◀ SINCE THE PATTERN of a picket fence is naturally repetitious, do something decorative to set the gate apart. Here, the heights of the gate pickets are varied, making the entrance easier for visitors to see and enter through.

Picket Fence Patterns

AN INVITING PICKET FENCE is a time-honored enclosure for a small front yard or garden. Picket fences are made of flat, evenly spaced slats nailed top and bottom to horizontal railings. Like most wood fences, picket fences can be constructed in sections that attach to posts mounted in the ground.

Picket tops are easy to cut into countless shapes to make the fence more ornamental; diamond point, round, and acorn are some of the most common designs. The slats also lend themselves to decorative cutouts, such as notches, circles, or squares.

Although vinyl is available, wood is still the most attractive material for picket fences. Choose a good-quality, water-resistant wood such as cedar, and take care that your pickets don't touch the ground. The posts, which will be in contact with the ground, should be pressure-treated to prevent rot. Keep a solid-wood fence sealed or painted, and it will reward you with years of service.

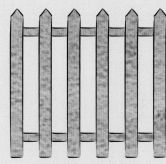

Diamond point

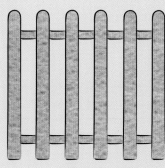

Round

Acorn

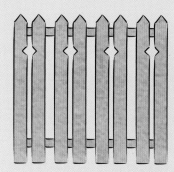

Diamond points with cutouts

▶ A FORMAL GATE is the perfect opening statement for a formal house. Centering the gate in line with the front door gives this property a complete sense of balance. To create a well-designed gate, look to details on your house. These gate posts are modeled on the columns around the front door.

◄ SOMETIMES TWO FENCES are better than one. A low stone wall provides support for a sloping yard, while a picket fence adds the security of a front gate. By painting the picket fence white, the homeowners brightened up their home by calling attention to the color of the house trim.

► AN ADOBE HOUSE all but calls out for an adobe fence. While this enclosure is especially tall to provide privacy, a lower wall could work in a more expansive setting. A bold arch clearly marks the entrance to the interior courtyard, which is visible through the novel metal gate.

▲ A WIDE GATE can make a high brick or stone wall less intimidating. This wood-plank gate fits snugly under an unusual brick archway that ties the gate in to the fence, spanning a double-width opening. The gate can be left invitingly ajar or securely locked.

WALLS

▲ WALLS CAN BE of almost any height. This low stone wall encloses a lush courtyard planted with shrubs, a spreading evergreen, and a flowering tree. The wall is low enough to make a cozy spot for wandering without losing contact with the yard beyond.

◀ WALLS FINISH OFF NEATLY with pillars that are slightly higher than the wall itself. This pair is topped with planters and provides crisp definition between a gravel driveway and the flagstone path leading to the house.

▶ A PATH LEADING THROUGH
a stone and mortar wall crosses
a dry stone bed, or arroyo, meant
to resemble a river. While the tan
and gray stones in the wall suggest the solidity of land, the blue
stones in the arroyo suggest water.

◀ TIERED WALLS—one high,
one low—come to the rescue
of a house that's both close to
the sidewalk and high above it.
The space between the two
walls makes an ideal planting
bed. Painting the walls white
helps set off colors and textures
in the plantings.

PERGOLAS

▲ AN ARBOR IS A SMALL VERSION of a pergola that arches over a door or gate. Although arbors are largely decorative, they can also support growing plants. This arbor encourages a rose-bush covered with pink blossoms to twine around its exposed rafters.

▲ A PERGOLA—a flat-roofed, openwork structure—is an ideal way to add pizzazz to a garden gate. The open rafters let in air and sunlight but are sturdy enough to support climbing vines that create a restful, shady space underneath.

▶ EVEN THOUGH PERGOLAS are typically open at the top, you can also include a covered section to provide extra shade or shelter. A sitting area at the juncture of this walkway and courtyard provides a good spot to escape a sudden shower or await a ride.

▲ IF YOU WANT TO CREATE SHADE along a walk but don't want to cover the area with a roof, build an extended pergola. This one is supported by rounded columns and screened by latticework with circular openings.

▲ THIS UNUSUALLY ORNATE FENCE incorporates two pergolas into its design—one over the gate and another over an interior walkway. The rafters that lie flat on top of the pergola repeat the pattern of the square, slender spindles grouped together in twos and threes in the fence, tying the two structures together.

Driveways

WHETHER YOUR DRIVEWAY IS LONG OR SHORT, it should be an asset to your house. Just like a walkway, a driveway usually needs maintenance and a refreshing of the surface material every few years. Cracked concrete, grass sprouting through asphalt, and gravel that is patchy in places can all severely compromise your home's appearance.

A driveway should be functional, too—at least 11 ft. wide and long enough for a driver to pull in safely from the street or to back out. Give some thought to the path your drive takes on its way to the house or garage: Straight or gently curving is usually best, with a flared entry where the drive meets the street. Consider, too, whether you want to include room for more than one parking space as part of the driveway or a turnaround space somewhere along the drive.

Finally, if your lot is small, don't overdo it: Keep the size of the driveway in scale with the house.

▶ LONG APPROACHES can be charming ones. If your drive is especially long, try to tie it to the landscape that it passes through. Edge it with shrubs or trees, or allow grass to grow between the tire tracks, for example.

▲ STONE PAVERS MAKE A DURABLE, easy-care surface for a driveway or parking area. Be sure to choose pavers that are intended for exterior use and that can bear weight.

◀ A CURVING DRIVEWAY will allow your house to shine upon approach, rather than calling attention to the garage. If you have enough space, place the parking area behind your house. This will allow you to create a driveway that doesn't threaten to visually dominate your home.

MATERIALS FOR DRIVEWAYS

◀ IF YOUR GARAGE IS ATTRACTIVE, the drive itself needn't stand out. It's important to keep the surface of the driveway in good repair, though: A few cracks or weeds sprouting through the asphalt can undermine the appearance of the rest of your property.

▼ EXPANSES OF BLACK ASPHALT can be visually overwhelming if they are in the front of a house. This asphalt drive, however, unifies the house and the garage. To further tie the driveway to the nearby architecture, the owner wisely chose a paint scheme that harmonizes with the shade of the asphalt.

▲ A CHIPPED-STONE DRIVEWAY next to a flagstone walk has a pebbly texture that complements the shingled exterior of this house. The drive is also edged with low pavers, which help keep the loose material where it belongs, rather than in the yard.

Driveway Paving Materials

DRIVEWAYS CAN BE PAVED with almost any material that drains well and stays more or less in place. The most durable materials include asphalt, concrete, pavers, and gravel, a medium that can vary from pea size to small stones.

- ASPHALT is a petroleum byproduct that arrives as a ready-to-spread hot mix. The hot mix is compacted by heavy rollers to create a smooth surface that should wear for years. Asphalt works well in cooler climates (the black color absorbs heat and can speed up snow and ice melt). It's less popular in warmer climates, where it can soften and develop ruts or gouges when it's exposed to high temperatures.

- CONCRETE is a mixture of sand, gravel, and cement that's poured in place. The surface is smoothed or brushed before it cures. Able to withstand extreme heat, it's the paving material of choice in hot climates. Concrete can also be pigmented, giving you a range of color choices. It can be subjected to any number of decorative treatments before it's fully cured, including stamping or etching to create interesting patterns like faux brick or stone.

- PAVERS are man-made stones that resemble either stone or brick. Made of clay and other natural materials, they are engineered to resist cracking in all types of weather extremes including freeze/thaw cycles and dry heat. Pavers are more expensive than either asphalt or concrete and cost more to install because they are laid by hand in interlocking patterns. If you like the look, however, this durable material will last indefinitely.

- GRAVEL is the least expensive material for driveways. Made of crushed, chipped, or natural stone, it comes in various sizes and colors. Gravel works well in cold or hot climates, but it needs to be refreshed with new gravel fairly often, particularly if the gravel is especially small (pea gravel). To keep gravel where you want it, consider adding a section of pavers, concrete, or asphalt at the turn-in to the driveway and alongside the edges of the drive. This will help keep the gravel from jumping out of its bed into the street and yard.

▶ KEPT NEATLY IN CHECK by a low wall and mulched planting beds, this gravel driveway makes an attractive approach. Because it is porous and allows water to percolate through to the soil layer, gravel works well in areas where rainwater tends to pond or cause flooding.

▲ BRICK PAVERS OFFER A **broad** range of natural earth colors that make them a beautiful choice for a driveway. The bricks can be laid in just as many patterns as a brick path, too, from traditional running bond to basket weave.

▶ STONE PAVERS IN A LIGHT GRAY color are an excellent choice for a driveway with a slightly below-grade garage. While asphalt would also be a good choice, a loose material like gravel wouldn't work here because it would tend to spread into the garage.

GRAVEL IS THE LEAST-EXPENSIVE paving material for driveways, but it needs frequent replenishing to keep the surface crisp and even. Edging the drive with a stone border can help keep the gravel in place and provide a barrier against creeping grass.

▲ THIS DRIVEWAY IS PAVED with a combination of materials. To handle the wear and tear of traffic, the owners put the most durable material on the tire tracks. They provided contrast by using gravel (a material, like grass, that drains well) as a supporting player.

◄ ASPHALT DRIVEWAYS are easy to install and last for many years. The material doesn't need an edge treatment and can be installed flush against a sidewalk, making it a good choice where easy accessibility is a factor.

▲ AN UNPAVED DRIVEWAY with grass growing between the tire tracks recalls a more relaxed era when cars were used less frequently. There's no rule that says you can't leave room for grass in a driveway, but you will have to cut it occasionally.

Matching Driveway to House Style

C HOOSE A MATERIAL FOR YOUR DRIVE that either complements some aspect of the house or contrasts with it in a pleasing way. For instance, brick pavers might seem like a natural choice for a red brick house, but the double whammy of brick drive and brick house might be overwhelming. A material of a different color—gray or black asphalt, light brown or gray gravel, or blue stone pavers—might give your drive just the lift it needs. Another trick is to match the color of the paving material to the color of the roof shingles, since there's a good chance the shingles already comple- ment your home's exterior and provide a little contrast to the siding color.

◄ A BED OF STONE GRAVEL appears to flow like a river between stone embedded in the ground. The material is a good choice because it shares an affinity with both the natural landscape and the gray color of the roof.

▲ IF YOUR YARD is big enough to accommodate one, a circular driveway can be especially useful because it allows vehicles to safely reverse direction. Because circular drives cover so much territory, they work best in yards with enough room for a dedicated parking area separate from areas for play and relaxation.

◄ EDGING AN EXPANSE OF ASPHALT with stone pavers gives a driveway a more permanent, finished look. The pavers gracefully mark the transition between the drive and the lawn. Since they are solid and stable, they also help prevent erosion at the edges of the asphalt.

Garages

ALMOST EVERY HOUSE seems to have a garage these days—with anywhere from one to three bays. Because garage bays tend to be wide and uniform in style, there's a danger that what many Americans regard as the ultimate necessity can overwhelm the appearance of an otherwise desirable house.

There are many ways to conceal or improve the appearance of a garage, even one with multiple bays. The design of the garage door, the placement of the garage within the façade, and well-chosen paint colors can make any garage better looking, if not exactly a thing of beauty. And if you are considering adding a garage as part of an addition or style makeover, by all means consider the design impact of this new structure with as much care as the rest of your home. A garage should complement a house, not dominate it.

▲ BECAUSE IT'S ON the lowest level, a townhouse garage tends to be less noticeable than other types of garages. The owner of this house further disguised its presence by adding a columned porch that doubles as the garage entry.

◄ TO MAKE AN ATTACHED GARAGE blend in with the rest of your house, paint it either the color of your house or the color of the house trim. Or add an accent that echoes the style of the home, like the arch over this garage door.

▲ A GARAGE THAT'S SET APART from the main house and matches it in style often has as much curb appeal as the house itself. This one is set behind the house, eliminating any possibility that it will appear overwhelming and visually dominate the nearby house.

► CARPORTS ARE A SHADY alternative to an enclosed garage in warmer climates, where sun and rain do more damage than ice and cold. A car parked outdoors is also more accessible. This area does double duty as a patio.

▼ TO MAKE THE MOST of the interior of a stand-alone garage, put the stairs to the second floor on the outside of the building. Nicely finished with a balustrade and capped posts, these include entry porches on the ground and second levels.

► SINCE A FREESTANDING GARAGE is as big as a small house, it makes sense to create finished space on the second floor. Options include space for an office, guest quarters, or an apartment for rental income.

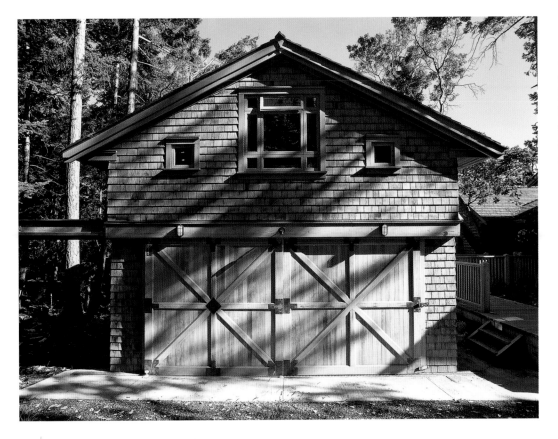

◀ THESE SLIDING GARAGE DOORS are decorated with diagonal cross bars to form an attractive pattern. Upstairs, the builder has created a variation on the cross-bar theme by adding a decorative grid at right angles to a large window.

IN THE DETAILS

Hiding Garbage Cans

K EEP YOUR TRASH and recycling bins out of sight—behind the house or tucked away in the garage if possible. If the trash must be kept out front, disguise or hide it with a screen, small shed, or partially enclosed fence. While you can build your own screen with materials from a home supply or builder's store, be on the lookout for ready-made screens and kits, which can save you time and money.

▶ HIDE YOUR TRASH BARREL until pick-up day with a freestanding screen in teak or cypress. The latticework on this ready-made screen conceals the barrel, yet allows for plenty of ventilation.

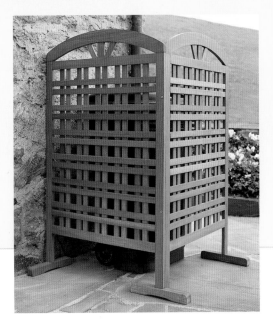

▲ TUCK GARBAGE CANS away in a small storage shed. This one is finished with sturdy doors and locks, a must in areas where garbage-loving animals like raccoons are a problem.

TRADITIONAL GARAGES

▲ TRIM COLOR applied to smaller features like windowsills and eaves shouldn't overwhelm the ground color when it's painted on a large feature like a garage door. Here, a white garage door gives a slate-blue house some much-needed contrast; a bolder color would have looked out of place.

▲ THE GARAGE DOORS on this reproduction of a vintage carriage house open manually. For far less money than a custom door, however, you can achieve the same look with a convenient fold-up door that automatically opens at the touch of a button.

▶ JUST BECAUSE A GARAGE is a utilitarian space doesn't mean it has to lack style. This freestanding shingled garage and workshop is loaded with detail, including the diagonal cross braces on the doors and window shutters and the dividers in the windows, accented in red paint.

Garage Door Designs

Until recently, most garage door styles resembled huge blank walls that had nothing to do with the rest of the house. You can still buy one of these unsightly doors, but for about the same amount of money, you can install a door that's much better suited to your house in terms of style, character, and paint-color combinations.

The best of the new generation of garage doors break the blank rectangular door into vertical sections that make it look as though the door swings or folds open. The simplest of these styles highlights the top of the door with a row of window panes (a). In a slightly more complicated version, the door appears to be divided into three vertical panels, each topped with its own window (b). A classic look is the carriage-house style, which features texturing or actual wood strips or paneling that makes it look as though the door swings open at the center. (c) Carriage-house styles that add windows at the top (d) take the illusion even further.

You can order a garage door in naturally finished or stained wood colors or in a paint-color combination that matches the ground and trim colors on your house. The design possibilities are limited only by your imagination.

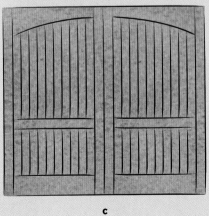

a

b

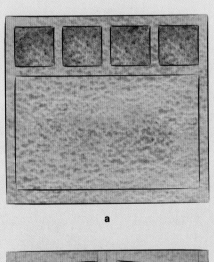

c

d

MULTIPLE GARAGES

▲ A TWO-BAY GARAGE can dominate a house if it isn't kept in scale. This one works because the wood doors blend well with other colors on the house. The garage also appears to step back from the main part of the house, making it less of an overpowering presence.

▶ ALTHOUGH THESE DOORS MATCH, one is staggered slightly behind the other. This staggered design not only prevents the garage from overwhelming the house, but also makes the house more interesting architecturally. Varying the placement of the garage doors also makes it easier to pull a car in and out of each bay.

◀ A STEEPLY PITCHED ROOF gives some variation to a double-bay garage with a bonus room upstairs. In spite of the steep slope, there's room overhead for twin beds, a small living area, and even a bathroom with shower.

▲ LIGHTS FOR A GARAGE don't have to be fancy, but for safety reasons, they should be bright enough to outline the door opening. Here, caged lights with flared shades cast light through the triple-pane windows, helping to illuminate the interior garage space at night.

◀ ANOTHER WAY TO eliminate monotony when there are multiple garage bays is to vary the rooflines. Here, the roof over the largest door is a gable, while the one over the other two doors is a shed roof. Setting back the two smaller bays also helps keep the garage from dominating the space.

▶ WHENEVER TWO OR MORE garage bays are grouped together, look for a way to break up the monotony. One time-honored method is to add architectural ornament: The curving cross-brace detail in this gable draws the eye away from the two bays but at the same time links both of them together.

▲ THE OWNERS OF THIS NEW shingled home came up with an inventive way to incorporate a double-bay garage without extensive blasting of the surrounding bedrock. The solution was to turn the garage at a 45-degree angle, which kept site costs in check.

A Garage Makeover

WHEN A NEW JERSEY couple purchased this tiny Cape, it was just big enough for two. Once a baby was due, however, the architect-owner began to think about the "bigger picture." A new garage was part of an expansion that more than tripled the size of the house. The owner kept the feel of the original Cape and transformed the cramped side entry into a larger breezeway that connects the house to the new garage.

The garage is linked to the remodeled house architecturally, with some important style differences that help keep it subordinate to the main house and also identify its function. The diagonal cross braces on the garage doors make it abundantly clear which part of the house is for cars and which is for people.

▲ AT 600 SQ. FT., this tiny Cape lacked a lot more than a garage before it was remodeled. The cramped side entry set back from the main part of the house, however, was the germ of an idea for a connecting breezeway to the new garage.

▲ ALTHOUGH THE ROOF PITCH on both the house and garage are closely matched, details in the top of the gables vary slightly: There are fish-scale shingles under the peak of the roof on the house, while a standing-seam tin detail appears on the garage.

◄ ALTHOUGH ALL THREE of these garage doors match and are arranged in a line, the interesting shapes of the surrounding stucco architecture provide some visual relief. The fact that one of the doors is slightly wider than the other two single-car doors beside it is another variation that keeps the garage from looking dull.

Resources

BOOKS AND MAGAZINES

One of the most thoughtful architects writing about the home today is Sarah Susanka, a regular contributor to *Fine Homebuilding* and *Inspired House* magazines, published by The Taunton Press. She is the author of a growing library of books, including two that you may find especially useful when considering ways to improve your home's curb appeal. They are *Not So Big Solutions for Your Home* (The Taunton Press, 2002) and *Home By Design: Inspiration for Transforming House into Home* (The Taunton Press, 2004). For information, contact The Taunton Press, 63 South Main St., Newtown, CT 06470, (800) 477-8727; www.taunton.com.

A great resource to get you thinking about individual elements that can make or break your home's appearance is Dennis Wedlick's *Good House Parts: Creating a Great Home Piece by Piece* (The Taunton Press, 2003). Although the scope of the book covers the entire house inside and out, you'll find plenty of ideas to improve your home's façade.

One of the most challenging aspects of *Taunton's Curb Appeal Idea Book* was trying to cover landscaping in a single chapter. If this is an area that particularly interests you, here are some suggestions for additional research.

For pure inspiration along with practical planting suggestions, there is no better source than the books of Ken Druse, which include *The Natural Garden* (Clarkson Potter, 1988), *The Natural Shade Garden* (Clarkson Potter, 1992), and any of Ken Druse's Natural Garden Guides: *Eighty Great Natural Shade Garden Plants* (Clarkson Potter, 1992, 1997), *80 Great Natural Garden Plants* (Three Rivers Press, 1997), and *80 Great Natural Habitat Plants* (Three Rivers Press, 1998). Although a number of these books are several years old, they're still available from online sources like amazon.com and abebooks.com.

For a more idea-based approach, among the best sources are *Taunton's Front Yard Idea Book*, by Jeni Webber (The Taunton Press, 2002) and *Landscaping Your Home: Creative Ideas from America's Best Gardeners*, by Lee Anne White, editor (The Taunton Press, Inc. 2001). And if you are an avid gardener, consider subscribing to *Fine Gardening*, also published by The Taunton Press.

DESIGNERS AND ARCHITECTS

The following is a partial list of professionals whose designs appear in this book.

Alden House
520 Aragon Blvd.
San Mateo, CA 94402
(650) 343-6446
www.Aldenhouse.net

Goodman Landscape Design
140 Montrose Rd.
Berkeley, CA 94707
(510) 528-8950
www.Goodmanlandscape.com

Huestis–Tucker Architects
2349 Whitney Ave.
Hamden, CT 06518
(203) 248-1007
www.huestistucker.com

Karreman & Associates
231 Gowen Pl. N.W.
Bainbridge Island, WA 98110
(206) 842-1253
www.karreman.com

WESKETCH Architects
1932 Long Hill Rd.
Millington, NJ 07946
(908) 647-8200
www.wesketch.com

SOURCES FOR CURB APPEAL IDEAS

While there are literally hundreds of sources for doors, windows, hardware, landscape lighting, and other exterior details for your home locally and nationally, some are easier to find than others. Here are a few suggestions for some of those hard-to-find items.

Doors and Windows

Andersen Windows & Doors
100 Fourth Ave. N.
Bayport, MN 55003-1096
(651) 264-5150
www.andersenwindows.com

Architectural Traditions
9280 E. Old Vail Rd.
Tucson, AZ 85747
(520) 574-7374
www.architecturaltraditions.com

International Door & Latch
1455 Westec Dr.
Eugene, OR 97402
(541) 686-5647
www.internationaldoor.com

Kolbe & Kolbe Millwork Co.
1323 S. 11th Ave.
Wausau, WI 54401
(715) 842-5666,
www.kolbe-kolbe.com

Loewen
77 Hwy. 52 W., Box 2260
Steinbach, Manitoba
Canada R5G 1B2
(800) 563-9367
www.Loewen.com

Touchstone Woodworks
P.O. Box 112
Ravenna, OH 44266
(330) 297-1313
www.touchstonewoodworks.com

Upstate Door Inc.
26 Industrial St.
Warsaw, NY 14509
(800) 570-8283
www.upstatedoor.com

Siding

Granville Manufacturing
Rte. 100
Granville, VT 05747
(802) 767-4747
www.woodsiding.com

NewSiding
42 Ladd St.
East Greenwich, RI 02818
www.New-siding.com

Shakertown Cedar Shingles
P.O. Box 400
1200 Kerron St.
Winlock, WA 98596
(800) 426-8970
www.shakertown.com

Roofing Materials and Details

Art of Rain
Vladimir Sumchenko
2313 NW 146th St.
Vancouver, WA 98685
(360) 891-6540
www.artofrain.com

The Bungalow Gutter Bracket Co.
P.O. Box 22144
Lexington, KY 40522
(859) 335-1555
www.bungalowgutterbracket.com

CertainTeed
P.O. Box 860
Valley Forge, PA 19482
(800) 782-8777
www.certainteed.com

McElroy Metal
1500 Hamilton Rd.
Bossier City, LA 71111
(888) 245-3696
www.mcelroymetal.com

Met-Tile
1745 Monticello Ct.
Ontario, CA 91761
(909) 947-0311
www.met-tile.com

The Tile Man
133 Hayfield Ct.
Wilmington, NC 28405
(866) 686-9394
www.thetileman.com

Shutters

Timberlane Woodcrafters
197 Wissahickon Ave.
North Wales, PA 19454
(800) 250-2221
www.timberlane.com

Garage Doors

Designer Doors™
183 E. Pomeroy St.
River Falls, WI 54022
(800) 241-0525
www.designerdoors.com

Summit Door
1233 Enterprise Ct.
Corona, CA 92882
(888) 768-3667
www.summitdoor.com

Hardware

Atlas Homewares
326 Mira Loma Avenue
Glendale, CA 91204
(818) 240-3500

House Number Connection
2525 E. 29th St., 10B
(509) 535-5098
Spokane, WA 99223
www.housenumber
connection.com

Liz's Antique Hardware
453 S. La Brea
Los Angeles, CA 90036
(323) 939-4403
www.lahardware.com

Nostalgic Warehouse®
4661 Monaco St.
Denver, CO 80216
(800) 522-7336
www.nostalgicwarehouse.com

Two Cats Co.
422 Mackenzie Pl.
Metamora, IL 61548
(309) 383-4430
www.door-knocker.com

Exterior Lighting

Arroyo Craftsman
4509 Little John St.
Baldwin Park, CA 91706
(800) 400-2776
www.arroyo-craftsman.com

B-K Lighting
40429 Brickyard Dr.
Madera, CA 93638
(559) 438-5800
www.bklighting.com

Farrey's Wholesale Hardware
1850 N.E. 146th St.
North Miami, FL 33181
(888) 854-5483
www.farreys.com/lighting/

Rejuvenation
1100 S.E. Grand Ave.
Portland, OR 97214
(503) 238-1900
www.Rejuvenation.com

Tahoe Lighting®
P.O. Box 4467
Sparks, NV 89432
(775) 356-1980
www.tahoelighting.com

Porches

Vintage Woodworks
P.O. Box 39
Quinlan, TX 75474
(903) 356-2158
www.vintagewoodworks.com

Vixen Hill
69 E. Main St.
Elverson, PA 19520
(800) 423-2766
www.vixenhill.com

Fences and Pergolas

Dufferin Iron & Fencing
5100 Rutherford Rd.
Woodbridge, Ontario
Canada L4H 2T3
(866) 955-0355
www.dufferiniron.com

Frederick Fence Co.
1505 Tilco Dr.
Frederick, MD 21704
(800) 49-FENCE
www.frederickfence.com

Walpole Woodworkers
767 East St.
Walpole, MA 02081
(800) 394-1933
www.walpolewoodworkers.com

Paving Materials

Halquist Stone
P.O. Box 308
Sussex, WI 53089
(800) 255-8811
www.halquiststone.com

J.M. DeLullo
1247 Million Dollar Hwy.
Kersey, PA 15846
(814) 834-1914
www.jmdstones.com

Pine Hall Brick
P.O. Box 11044
Winston-Salem, NC 27116
(800) 334-8689
www.americaspremierpaver.com

Fountains

Oregon Copper Bowl
P.O. Box 5859
Eugene, OR 97405
(541) 485-9845
www.oregoncopperbowl.com

RainChains.com
8040 Remmet Avenue, Unit 7
Canoga Park, CA 91304
(888) 480-RAIN (7246)
(818) 347-6455
www.rainchains.com

Simply Fountains
10842 Farnam Dr., Suite 100
Omaha, NE 68154
(800) 901-8865
www.simplyfountains.com

Credits

CHAPTER 1

p. 4: Photo © Brian Vanden Brink

p. 6: (left) Photo © Grey Crawford; (right) Photo © Brian Vanden Brink

p. 7: Photo © Brian Vanden Brink

p. 8: (top) Photo © Chipper Hatter; (bottom) Photo © Brian Vanden Brink

pp. 9–11: Photos © Brian Vanden Brink

p. 12: Photo © Grey Crawford

p. 13: (top) Photo © Erik Kvalsvik; (bottom) Photo © Brian Vanden Brink

p. 14: Photo © Chipper Hatter

p. 15: Todd Caverly, photographer © 2005, Brian Vanden Brink photos

p. 16: (left) Photo by Charles Bickford, © The Taunton Press, Inc.; (right) Photo by Charles Miller, © The Taunton Press, Inc.

p. 17: Photo © 2005 Carolyn L. Bates/www.carolynbates.com

p. 18: Photos © Brian Vanden Brink

p. 19: Photo © 2005 Carolyn L. Bates/www.carolynbates.com

p. 20: Photos © Linda Svendsen

p. 21: (left) Photo © Lisa Goodman, Goodman Landscape Design; (right) Photo © Linda Svendsen

pp. 22–24: Photos © Brian Vanden Brink

p. 25: Photo © Chipper Hatter

p. 26: (top left) Photo © Brian Vanden Brink; (top right & bottom) Photos © Chipper Hatter

p. 27: (top) Photo © Brian Vanden Brink; (bottom) Photo © Chipper Hatter

CHAPTER 2

p. 28: Photo © Chipper Hatter

p. 30: Photo © Chipper Hatter

p. 31: Photos © Brian Vanden Brink

p. 32: (left & top right) Photos © Brian Vanden Brink; (bottom right) Photo © Chipper Hatter

p. 33: (top) Photo Chipper Hatter; (bottom) Photo © Linda Svendsen

p. 34: Photo © Brian Vanden Brink

p. 35: (top left) Photo © www.davidduncanlivingston.com; (top right) Photo by Charles Miller, © The Taunton Press, Inc.; (bottom) Photo © Brian Vanden Brink

p. 36: (top) Photo © Chipper Hatter; (bottom) Photo © Brian Vanden Brink

p. 37: (left) Photo © 2005 Carolyn L. Bates/www.carolynbates.com; (right) Photo © Chipper Hatter

p. 38: (top) Photo © Chipper Hatter; (bottom) Photo © Erik Kvalsvik

p. 39: (top) Photo © Linda Svendsen; (bottom) Photo © Brian Vanden Brink

p. 40: (left) Photo by Tom O'Brien, © The Taunton Press, Inc.; (right) Photo © Robert Perron

p. 41: (top) Photo © 2005 Carolyn L. Bates/www.carolynbates.com; (bottom) Photos courtesy The Tileman, Inc.

p. 42: (left) Photo by Charles Miller, © The Taunton Press, Inc.; (right) Photo © Brian Vanden Brink

p. 43: Photo © Chipper Hatter

p. 44: (top & bottom) Photos © Chipper Hatter; (center) Photo © Linda Svendsen

p. 45: (top) Photo © Brian Vanden Brink; (bottom) Photo by Charles Miller, © The Taunton Press, Inc.

p. 46: (left) Photo © www.davidduncanlivingston.com; (top right) Photo © Linda Svendsen; (bottom right) Photo by Charles Miller, © The Taunton Press, Inc.

p. 47: (top) Photo © Robert Perron; (bottom) Photo © William P. Wright

pp. 48–49: Photos © 2005 Carolyn L. Bates/www.carolynbates.com

p. 50: Photo © Frank Karreman

p. 51: Photo © Steve Keating

p. 52: (top) Photo © Lance Johnson; (bottom) Photo by Charles Miller, © The Taunton Press, Inc

p. 53: Photo © Brian Vanden Brink

pp. 54–55: Photos © Randy O'Rourke

p. 56: Photos © Chipper Hatter

p. 57: Photos © Howard Pruden

CHAPTER 3

p. 58: Photo © Linda Svendsen

p. 60: (top) Photo © Linda Svendsen; (bottom) Photo © Chipper Hatter

p. 61: (top) Photo © Chipper Hatter; (bottom) Photo © www.davidduncanlivingston.com

p. 62: (left) Photo courtesy Upstate Doors; (right) Photo © Linda Svendsen

p. 63: (top) photo © Randy O'Rourke; (bottom) Photo © Linda Svendsen

p. 64: Photo © William P. Wright

p. 65: (left) Photo © Brian Vanden Brink; (top right) Photo by Chris Green, © The Taunton Press, Inc.; (bottom right) Photo © Chipper Hatter

p. 66: Photos © Ken Gutmaker

p. 67: (top) Photo © Brian Vanden Brink; (bottom) Photo © www.davidduncanlivingston.com

p. 68: (left) Photo © Paul Bardagjy; (right) Photo © Linda Svendsen

p. 69: (top left) Photo © Brian Vanden Brink; (top right) Photo by Charles Miller, © The Taunton Press, Inc.; (bottom) Photo © www.davidduncanlivingston.com

p. 70: (left) Photo by Charles Miller, © The Taunton Press, Inc.; (right) Photo © Brian Vanden Brink

p. 71: (top) Photo © Ken Gutmaker; (bottom) Photo © Chipper Hatter

p. 72: (top) Photo © Brian Vanden Brink; (bottom) Photo © Linda Svendsen

p. 73: (top) Photo by Charles Miller, © The Taunton Press, Inc.; (bottom) Photo © Brian Vanden Brink

p. 74: (top) Photo © Grey Crawford; (bottom) Photo © Ken Gutmaker

p. 75: (left) Photo © Randy O'Rourke; (right) Photo © 2005 Carolyn L. Bates/www.carolynbates.com

p. 76: (top left & right) Photos © Linda Svendsen; (bottom) Photo © Chipper Hatter

p. 77: (top) Photo © Linda Svendsen; (bottom) Photo © 2005 Carolyn L. Bates/www.carolynbates.com

p. 78: Photo © Erik Kvalsvik

p. 79: (top left & right) Photos © Linda Svendsen; (bottom left & right) Photos © William P. Wright

p. 80: (left) Photo by Charles Miller, © The Taunton Press, Inc.; (top right) Photo © Chipper Hatter; (bottom right) Photo © Linda Svendsen

p. 81: (top) Photo © Brian Vanden Brink; (bottom) Photo © Jason McConathy

p. 82: (top) Photo courtesy Arroyo Craftsman; (bottom left) Photo © Evan Sklar; (bottom right) Photo © Ken Gutmaker

p. 83: (bottom) Photo courtesy B-K Lighting

p. 84: (top) Photos courtesy Atlas Homewares; (bottom left & center) Photos courtesy Rain Chains, Inc.; (bottom right) Photo © Vladimir Sumchenko

p. 85: (top & bottom left) Photos © Vladimir Sumchenko; (top & bottom right) Photos courtesy Atlas Homewares

p. 86: (top) Photo © Linda Svendsen; (bottom) Photo © Brian Vanden Brink

p. 87: Photo © 2005 Carolyn L. Bates/www.carolynbates.com

p. 88: (left) Photo © Robert Perron; (right) Photo © Brian Vanden Brink

p. 89: (top) Photo © www.davidduncanlivingston.com; (bottom left) Photo © 2005 Carolyn L. Bates/www.carolynbates.com; (bottom right) Photo © Erik Kvalsvik

p. 90: (left) Photo © Brian Vanden Brink; (right) Photo ©www.davidduncanlivingston.com

p. 91: (top) Photo © 2005 Carolyn L. Bates/www.carolynbates.com; (bottom) Photo by Chris Green, © The Taunton Press, Inc.

p. 92: (top) Photo © Brian Vanden Brink; (bottom) Photo © Grey Crawford

p. 93: (top) Photo © Brian Vanden Brink; (bottom left) Photo © Chipper Hatter; (bottom right) Photo by Charles Miller, © The Taunton Press, Inc.

p. 94: Photo by Andy Engel, © The Taunton Press, Inc.

p. 95: (top left) Photo © 2005 Carolyn L. Bates/www.carolyn-bates.com; (bottom left) Photo by Charles Miller, © The Taunton Press, Inc.; (right) Photo by Daniel S. Morrison, © The Taunton Press, Inc.

p. 96: Photo © www.daviddun-canlivingston.com

p. 97: (top & bottom right) Photos © Chipper Hatter; (bottom left) Photo © 2005 Carolyn L. Bates/www.carolynbates.com

p. 98: (left) Photo © Linda Svendsen; (top right) Photo © Chipper Hatter; (bottom right) Photo © 2005 Carolyn L. Bates/www.carolynbates.com

p. 99: (top) Photo © Robert Perron; (bottom) Photo © Brian Vanden Brink.

CHAPTER 4

p. 100: Photo © Chipper Hatter

pp. 102–103: Photos © Brian Vanden Brink

p. 104: Photo © Linda Svendsen; p. 105: (top left) Photo © Brian Vanden Brink; (top right) Photo © John Gruen; (bottom) Photo by Charles Bickford, © The Taunton Press, Inc.

p. 106: (top) Photo by Steve Aitken, © The Taunton Press, Inc.; (bottom) Photo © Lee Anne White p. 107: (top) Photo © Chipper Hatter; (bottom) Photo © Lee Anne White

p. 108: (left) Photo © Chipper Hatter; (top right & bottom) Photos © Linda Svendsen

p. 109: (top) Photo © Robert Perron; (bottom) Photo © Brian Vanden Brink

p. 110: (top) Photo © www.david-duncanlivingston.com; (bottom) Photo © Lee Anne White

p. 111: (top) Photo by Todd Meier, © The Taunton Press, Inc.; (bottom) Photo © Linda Svendsen

p. 112: (top left) Photo by Michelle Gervais, © The Taunton Press, Inc.; (top center & top right) Photos by Todd Meier, © The Taunton Press, Inc.; (bottom) Photos by Virginia Small, © The Taunton Press, Inc.

p. 113: (top) Photo © Lee Anne White; (bottom) Photo by Evan Sklar, © The Taunton Press, Inc.

p. 114: (top) Photo © Brian Vanden Brink; (bottom) Photo © Robert Perron

p. 115: (top) Photo © Brian Vanden Brink; (bottom) Photo © Chipper Hatter

p. 116: Photo © Linda Svendsen

p. 117: Photos © Robert Perron

p. 118: Photos © Lisa Goodman, Goodman Landscape Design

p. 119: (top) Photo © Ken Gutmaker; (bottom) Photo by Virginia Small, © The Taunton Press, Inc.

p. 120: Photos © Brian Vanden Brink

p. 121: (top) Photo by Steve Silk, © The Taunton Press, Inc.; (bottom) Photo © Linda Svendsen

p. 122: (top & bottom left) Photos © Chipper Hatter; (bottom right) Photo © www.daviddunclanlivingston.com

p. 123: (top) Photo © Brian Vanden Brink; (bottom) Photo by Roe A. Osborn, © The Taunton Press, Inc.

p. 124: (left & top) Photos © 2005 Carolyn L. Bates/www.carolyn-bates.com; (bottom) Photo © Lee Anne White

p. 125: (left) Photo © Lee Anne White; (right) Photo © Chipper Hatter

p. 126: (left & top right) Photos © Brian Vanden Brink; (bottom) Photo © Linda Svendsen

p. 127: Photos © Robert Perron

p. 128: (top) Photo © Linda Svendsen; (left) Photo © Robert Perron; (right) Photo © Brian Vanden Brink

p. 129: (left) Photo © Brian Vanden Brink; (right) Photo © Robert Perron

p. 130: (top) Photo © Rob Karosis; (bottom) Photo © Chipper Hatter

p. 131: (top) Photo © Mike Moore; (bottom) Photo by Andy Engel, © The Taunton Press, Inc.

p. 132: (top) Photo © Chipper Hatter; (bottom) Photo © 2005 Carolyn L. Bates/www.carolyn-bates.com

p. 133: (left) Photo by Lee Anne White, © The Taunton Press, Inc.; (right) Photo © Chipper Hatter

p. 134: (left) Photo by Lee Anne White, © The Taunton Press, Inc.; (right) Photo © Chipper Hatter

p. 135: (top) Photo by Scott Gibson, © The Taunton Press, Inc.; (bottom) Photo © Lee Anne White.

CHAPTER 5

p. 136: Todd Caverly, photographer © 2005, Brian Vanden Brink photos

p. 138: (top) Photo © Linda Svendsen; (bottom) Photo © Robert Perron

p. 139: (top) Photo © Brian Vanden Brink; (bottom) Photo by Andy Engel, © The Taunton Press, Inc.

p. 140: (top) Photo © Linda Svendsen; (bottom) Photo © Brian Vanden Brink

p. 141: (top) Photo © Brian Vanden Brink; (bottom) Photo © Chipper Hatter; (right) Photo © Linda Svendsen

p. 142: Photo © Brian Vanden Brink

p. 143: (top) Photo © Brian Vanden Brink; (right & bottom) Photos © Chipper Hatter

pp. 144–145: Photos © Lee Anne White

p. 146: (left & top right) Photos © Brian Vanden Brink; (bottom right) Photo © 2005 Carolyn L. Bates/www.carolynbates.com

p. 147: (top) Photo © Robert Perron; (bottom) Photo © Linda Svendsen

p. 148: Photo © Brian Vanden Brink

p. 149: (top) Photo © Chipper Hatter; (bottom) Photo by Roe A. Osborn, © The Taunton Press, Inc.

p. 150: (top) Photo © Robert Perron; (bottom left) Photo © Brian Vanden Brink; (bottom right) Photo © 2005 Carolyn L. Bates/www.carolynbates.com

p. 151: Photo © Lee Anne White

p. 152: (top) Photo © Robert Perron; (bottom) Photo © Brian Vanden Brink

p. 153: (top left) Photo © 2005 Carolyn L. Bates/www.carolyn-bates.com; (top right) Photo © Linda Svendsen; (bottom) Photo © Robert Perron

p. 154: Photo © Ken Gutmaker

p. 155: (top left & bottom) Photos © Lee Anne White; (top right) Photo © Rob Karosis

p. 156: (top) Photo © www.david-duncanlivingston.com; (bottom) Photo © Robert Perron

p. 157: Photo © Brian Vanden Brink

p. 158: (top) Photo © Mary Rezny; Architect: Brent Richards, Ross/Tarrant Architects, Inc., Lexington, KY; (bottom left) Photo by Andy Engel, © The Taunton Press, Inc.; Builder: Ken Troupe, Sudbury, ON; (bottom right) Photo by Andy Engel, © The Taunton Press, Inc.

p. 159: (top) Photo by Charles Miller, © The Taunton Press, Inc.; (bottom left) Photo courtesy Plow and Hearth; (bottom right) Photo by John Rickard, © The Taunton Press, Inc.

p. 160: (top left & bottom) Photos © Brian Vanden Brink; (top right) Photo by Chris Green, © The Taunton Press, Inc.

p. 162: (top) Photo © Linda Svendsen; (bottom) Photo © Chipper Hatter

p. 163: (top left) Photo by Roe A. Osborn, © The Taunton Press, Inc.; Mark Osburn & Wayne Clarke, Architects; (top right) Photo © Erik Kvalsvik; (bottom) Photo © Linda Svendsen

p. 164: (top) Photo © Robert Perron; (bottom) Photo © Ken Gutmaker

p. 165: (top left) Photo by William Kaufman, © The Taunton Press, Inc.; (top right) Photo © Ken Gutmaker; WESKETCH Architects; (bottom) Photo © Linda Svendsen.

For More Great Design Ideas, Look for These and Other Taunton Press Books wherever Books are Sold.